What the Future of Humanity Could Be!

THE AQUARIAN TEAM

BALBOA.
PRESS

A DIVISION OF HAY HOUSE

Balboa Press books may be ordered through booksellers or by contacting:

Balboa Press
A Division of Hay House
1663 Liberty Drive
Bloomington, IN 47403
www.balboapress.com
1-(877) 407-4847

Because of the dynamic nature of the Internet, any web addresses or links contained in this book may have changed since publication and may no longer be valid. The views expressed in this work are solely those of the authors and do not necessarily reflect the views of the publisher, and the publisher hereby disclaims any responsibility for them.

The authors of this book does not dispense medical advice or prescribe the use of any technique as a form of treatment for physical, emotional, or medical problems without the advice of a physician, either directly or indirectly. The intent of the authors is only to offer information of a general nature to help you in your quest for emotional and spiritual well-being. In the event you use any of the information in this book for yourself, which is your constitutional right, the authors and the publisher assume no responsibility for your actions.

Any people depicted in stock imagery provided by Thinkstock are models, and such images are being used for illustrative purposes only.
Certain stock imagery © Thinkstock.

ISBN: 978-1-4525-6156-1 (sc)
ISBN: 978-1-4525-6158-5 (hc)
ISBN: 978-1-4525-6157-8 (e)
Library of Congress Control Number: 2012920130

Printed in the United States of America

Balboa Press rev. date: 11/26/2012

In gratitude to our beloved teacher and instructor.

Contents

Illustrations

Full color versions of these images are available on our website and may be accessed through the BalboaPress online Bookstore at http://bookstore.balboapress.com/

Introduction

No one can deny that we presently live in a most interesting era. Everything moves so fast; it seems that we never have enough time to do everything, despite so much industrial and technological progress. Could we be living nine lives in one, like the whole cycle of a cat's life?

Some people's lives are overloaded; they keep running all the time while others are so overwhelmed by the advances of the last half century that they remain passive or barely scrape by. One thing for sure is that we cannot remain indifferent to the direction that humanity is taking—be it on a political, economic, social, ecological, or religious level. Where are we going at this speed? Toward progress or destruction? The planet has never been so populated. It is an incredible opportunity to be incarnated now because of the increasing speed and intensity of life. For some people, it is an interesting era; for others, it is a troubling one.

A new life is dawning and bringing about change—whether we like it or not. Aquarius pours out its energy, just as the sun radiates its light and warmth.

Master Aïvanhov said, "The beauty, splendor and harmony of the new life that will emerge [...] will be beyond anything imagined."[1]

This new era will definitely come, but it will most likely be after some difficult times. As we sense, nothing is stable anymore. There

---

1   Omraam Mikhaël Aïvanhov, *A New Dawn: Society and Politics in the Light of Initiatic Science*, Complete Works, Vol. 25, France, Prosveta S.A., ed. 1990, back cover.

will be more calling upon us. Let us be open to this call that will make the future of humanity a garden of paradise!

As you pursue this reading, you may feel something awakening in you. If so, we will have touched a sensitive chord within, a chord vibrating to these new currents that are about to allow humankind to find its true humanity, its divinity.

This book is the result of teamwork which, combined with the energy of Aquarius, helped bring it to fruition. Those involved could be described as disciples of a new life who are inspired by the teachings of philosophers and spiritual Masters such as Omraam Mikhaël Aïvanhov.

CHAPTER 1

Politics: Aristocracy, Democracy, and Synarchy

POLITICAL STAKES REGULARLY CHANGE, yet the world is still faced with the same problems that need to be resolved.

Political ideals are often replaced because, most likely, they are based solely on intellectual understanding. Oligarchy, aristocracy, monarchy, and democracy have often led countries to anarchy at one time or another.

What is missing within politics to bring security, peace, and growth to humankind?

People say, "The more things change, the more they stay the same." Politicians soak up the energies and ideas left by their predecessors, which is why the promises they make during campaigns often fall through. Their power remains limited to the economic circumstances and influences of those around them. As long as politicians are motivated by personal ambitions, vanity, interests, or power, they will not be able to offer any guarantee of peace or prosperity.

Hitler, Stalin, and other dictators in the modern world have exercised an incredible influence, and too many people, without discernment, have followed them at great personal cost. What were these people hoping for? They thought those political leaders were needed to meet an urgent need for change. Because they were not enlightened, they allowed themselves to be led to war and misery.

1

Even today, despots fill their pockets while their people live in misery and poverty.

Initiates see things from a different point of view than ordinary people do. They rise above human perceptions to see from the summit or the center. The opinions of most humans originate from a geocentric point of view; for instance, not so long ago, people believed the sun circled the earth. Initiates, on the contrary, consider everything from a heliocentric perspective, whereby the sun is the stable body around which planets revolve. Today, everyone accepts this reality from an astronomical perspective but not quite from a psychological or a psychic one. Initiates stand by truth alone.

When we perceive politics from the point of view of the Initiates, we realize that people often elect a president or governor depending on their own limitations and down-to-earth ideas rather than their aspirations and ideals.

> When the people of a country improve, heaven sends them enlightened rulers who bring them well-being and prosperity but, when they sink into evil ways, heaven sends a tyrant to rule over them. This is the law. It is important to know these laws.[2]

We all come from the same creator, which means that we all have the same physical and psychic structure. We all have a heart, an intellect, and willpower. We all have the same needs: happiness, love, and freedom. In addition, we are all inhabited by two natures: one personal and one impersonal, the "little self" and the "big self," or "personality" and "individuality." The *personality* wants everything for itself; it is basically egoistic and is always acting for its own benefit. By contrast, the *individuality* wants be of service; it is always altruistic, it gives out of selflessness. Therefore, politicians who are guided by their *personality* alone cannot avoid injustices or offer any guarantee of peace for their countries or the planet.

Many civilizations have disappeared—usually because personalities allowed certain human beings to dominate and enslave

---

2   Ibid, p. 41

others through violence. When politicians are inspired by their *individuality* and manifest generosity and wisdom, they become heads of government who are efficient, inspiring, reassuring, and thus beneficial to all their people.

> Before anyone can be a true political leader, he must have a profound knowledge of man and nature and a profound respect for divine law. Also, he must be free from all ambition, all personal passions.[3]

Aristocracy and Democracy

Some say that democracy corresponds to the stomach, belly, and sex, and that aristocracy is linked to the head. Intellectual faculties emanate from the brain. Left on their own, however, and under the influence of the personality, these faculties sometimes manage to succeed in the most pernicious projects.

In order to harness the tendencies of the *personality* for the benefit of the *individuality*, a strong desire to transform oneself and establish an inner aristocracy is paramount. In addition, knowledge of oneself is needed—not only at the physical and psychological levels but also at the psychic level. Acquiring the appropriate methods of work is another essential element. Finally, developing the knowledge and understanding of the laws that govern the universe, nature, and human beings is indispensable. The human structure displaying the head and brain above the other organs is an image and an indication of the process necessary to accomplish this work.

> As long as economists and politicians forget about the need for water and think that all they have to do to improve the situation is to set up a good organization, create new institutions and new structures or new administrative posts, the process of death and disintegration will continue. Whatever is done on the purely external, organizational level

---

3   Ibid. p. 230

will be ineffectual if nothing is done to ensure the flow of water [love]. This is why it is essential that there should be someone at the top who is rich in light, knowledge, and love, for then every branch and every department will know how to contribute to the success of the whole.[4]

The whole universe is built as a hierarchy and follows a well-established cosmic order; otherwise, all would be chaos. Most human beings are not aware of this cosmic order and the laws governing it; therefore, they cannot respect it. When people recognize their inner hierarchy, giving priority to the life of the soul and the spirit, and when they engage in the process of mastering their own thoughts, feelings, and actions, they will become masters of their own kingdom. They will do good wherever they go. Inspired by this noble hierarchy, politics will then follow in the form of a *synarchy*—the one model that the great Masters and Initiates support.

> The only valid form of politics is that of the Initiates who have studied human nature and know all its strengths and weaknesses, who know what it needs and what spiritual, emotional, moral and economic conditions are most conducive to its fulfillment. As long as this knowledge is lacking, politics can only lead to conflict.[5]

So, who are these Initiates and great Masters? In *The Great Initiates*, Édouard Schuré[6] describes them as a group of most evolved beings who have managed to discover the same realities of the invisible world. Rama, Krishna, Hermes, Moses, Orpheus, Pythagoras, Plato, and Jesus are only some of the remarkable beings he refers to. Each of them brought a knowledge and some methods corresponding to the era in which they lived.

---

4   Ibid. p. 232
5   Ibid. p. 231
6   Édouard Schuré, *The Great Initiates*, Steinerbooks, 1961

Materialization of their message, however, created separate religions, dividing one from the other. Nevertheless, in the world of ideas, these religions remain united in the same cause and work together for the advancement of humanity.

INNER UNITY: THE IDEA OF A PAN-EARTH

Freedom and inner unity go hand in hand. The less we control our thoughts, desires, and whims, the more we become enslaved. True freedom, according to the Sages, is the result of self-mastery.

A human being is based on the model of the cosmos and functions on those same principles. Unity between countries should begin with unity within oneself, amongst one's own organs. The heart does not beat for itself alone, and the stomach does not digest just for itself but for the well-being of the whole person. When an organ ceases to function for the overall health of the person, anarchy settles in and a tumor or a cancer appears.[7] Therefore, "Even physical health depends on obedience to this universal order—call it what you will: synarchy, hierarchy or divine monarchy." [8]

When all the organs work together for the harmony of a being, health prevails. Countries are also the organs of the planetary body, and when a country works only for itself, to the detriment of other countries, anarchy eventually follows. If all the countries worked together for the well-being of humanity, harmony would reign and a Pan-Earth would emerge. This is a concept we will cover later on.

Besides this organ interdependency, scientists also recognize the hierarchy of the different body systems: skeletal, muscular, circulatory, and nervous. Some leading edge scientists now include the auric system in this hierarchy—the one containing the waves of light and colors, which are the reflections of the thoughts and feelings of an individual.

---

7   This idea was presented by Omraam Mikhaël Aïvanhov during an interview on July 13, 1985 for the Live Aid international concert.

8   Omraam Mikhaël Aïvanhov, *A New Dawn: Society and Politics in the Light of Initiatic Science*, Complete Works, Vol. 25, France, Prosveta S.A., ed. 1990, p. 78.

But let's get back to this idea of hierarchy, for it is extremely useful for our inner life. If we know that everything — from the stones of the earth to God Himself—is linked hierarchically, and if we keep this structure constantly in mind, we are bound to act accordingly and do what is right, for we see that everything fits in to that order, that organization, that system. Hierarchy is a state of perfect harmony in which each element is in place. This applies in every domain and, if most human beings are so unhappy, it is because they do not respect this hierarchy. Their belly is where their head or their heart should be and vice versa. There is no order.[9]

The soul and the spirit represent the highest nature of a human being. They form the dot at the center of a circle where peace prevails. Recognizing this reality and connecting with the divine world nourishes our subtle bodies, gives a direction to our energies, and stabilizes any opposing currents.

Georg Feuerstein, in his work *The Mystery of Light*, writes:

The only way to heal ourselves and our ailing planet is by going to the root of the problem—which is our spiritual dislocation, our frivolous and by now habitual attitude of disregard for the Source of all life. We must recover our connection to the Divine, which alone can give us primal trust and the strength and wisdom to live our lives in harmony.[10]

Bringing unity within is the first task we must focus on in order to establish harmony. Initially, the head will make the decision to enter this process; the heart will then need to accept and feel; willpower

9   Ibid. p. 250
10   Georg Feuerstein, *The Mystery of Light, U.S.A.*, Passage Press, 1994, p. 257

will finally set everything into motion. Once we establish harmony and unity within, we are invited to realize it in the world:

> There are not many who are inwardly united. This is why we must work to make inner universal brotherhood a reality; we must work to unite human beings, peoples and nations and help them to attain that sublime consciousness of unity and a life of fulfillment and abundance, a life of inner prosperity.[11]

THE GOVERNMENT OF THE INITIATES: SYNARCHY

Initiates and great Masters believe that the governing model of the future will be based on the cosmic order, on the image of the universe. It will generate order, happiness, joy, and plenitude for all. Force, be it military or economic, will no longer be necessary.

> Hitherto human history has been a tragicomedy of tribal allegiance and, later, of national sovereignty, empire building, and capitalist or communist imperialism—all manifestations of the primitive urges to gain material security and exercise power over others. Aïvanhov saw world government as a political innovation that inevitably will be connected with humanity's spiritual maturity.[12]

At present, with the failure of communism and capitalism, and with so many countries going bankrupt, synarchy may appear like utopia. Many strongly believe, however, that synarchy will be the form of government eventually accepted because everything else will have failed.

---

11 Omraam Mikhaël Aïvanhov, *A New Dawn: Society and Politics in the Light of Initiatic Science*, Complete Works, Vol. 25, France, Prosveta S.A., Ed. 1990, p. 28.

12 Georg Feuerstein, *The Mystery of Light*, Passage Press 1994, p. 256

People will then be ready to be governed by this new system, a system that is above the many facets of the personality. Synarchy is based on eternal, unchangeable, and immutable laws and principles. The time will come when people will accept the truths taught by the great Masters and Initiates over the centuries; people will recognize that the human organization must follow the cosmic organization in order to guarantee the survival of the planet.

The coming of Aquarius brings about tremendous changes that will open up a new culture, a new civilization, and new politics—all of them based on the science of the Initiates and on synarchy. In the past, Ram, who had been instructed in the *initiatic science*[13] by Vashista, was able to install a Golden Age through synarchy; thanks to his knowledge and his forbearance, humanity lived in peace and abundance for many centuries.

> A synarchy form of government puts love, wisdom and truth in first place, and power and economic interests are seen as secondary in importance.[14]

This form of government already exists as the Marquis Saint-Yves D'Alveydre mentions in his book *La Mission de l'Inde.*[15] He explains in detail its formation and its operation in Agartha, the nearly impenetrable legendary kingdom at the center of the Earth. Thanks to his astral traveling ability, Saint-Yves d'Alveydre apparently visited that kingdom repeatedly. Ossendowki also describes the same governing system in his book *Beasts, Men and Gods.*[16]

---

13 The science based on the laws of the cosmos and on nature which all Initiates study, verify, and transmit to their disciples, thus the term *Initiatic Science*

14 Omraam Mikhaël Aïvanhov, *A New Dawn: Society and Politics in the Light of Initiatic Science,* Complete Works, Vol. 25, France, Prosveta S.A, ed. 1990, pp. 234–235.

15 Saint-Yves d'Alveydre, Mission de l'Inde en Europe, France, Belisane, 1981

16 Ferdinand Ossendowski, *"Beast Men and Gods"* New York: E. P. Dutton & Company, 1922.

Once human beings accept this system of government, all political, economic, and social problems will be resolved.

Thanks to synarchy, Earth will become a garden of paradise where all will live and act as brothers and sisters, as sons and daughters of the same father, God; as sons and daughters of the same mother, Mother Nature.

Exercise: Let us form links of light to help bring about a better world. In the first link, visualize yourself, then add your father, as he represents the head of your family (whatever opinion you have of him), then add the mayor of your city, followed by the head of the government of your country (whether you support that party or not, the goal here is to link ourselves with something sublime). Add the Regent of the planet, known as Sandalfon in the Kabala and then still higher up, the head of the solar system, the Sun or the Christ, as you prefer and, finally, the Lord or the Source of all life. Thus, we all form a chain where light circulates and all benefit.[17]

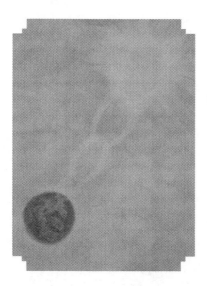

Links of Light

---

17 This exercise is based on a method given in the "Seven beads of the Rosary" by Omraam Mikhaël Aïvanhov, *The Splendour of Tiphareth*, Complete Works, Vol. 10, France, Prosveta S.A, ed. 1987, p. 66.

CHAPTER 2

Economy: To Take and To Give

WE ARE IN A world today where we hear that the most important thing is the economy. The stress that individuals are putting on themselves and on the earth is enormous. Most people are unhappy with the state and direction of the global economy.

Economy of itself is neither good nor bad. It is the ideas that govern it that are either good or bad, and thus make the economy move in one direction or another. The world today is so materialized that no one pays attention to this subtle, imponderable, aspect called intelligence, although intelligence is what guides those ideas which in turn allow the capitals, resources, imports, and exports to move.

We notice around the world a vast amount of debt, joblessness, unhappiness, and materialism. So many people are influenced by the insatiable thirst for money and for possessions. Nowadays, all forms of comfort are accessible, and new technological discoveries make life easier; yet, in spite of these inventions, people keep on pushing to acquire more and are not necessarily any happier because true happiness does not belong in possessions.

If the economy is not working properly, it is because it is based on the principle of materialism and credit. We borrow money against other borrowed money—with no real or tangible assets to support this principle.

Our banks and institutions take advantage of the working class by lending them money to a debt level that is near impossible to ever repay. They profit from the interests and are then able to leverage more money.

In many countries, the middle class is slowly disappearing with the outsourcing of good-paying jobs to countries that have lower wages and lower standards of living—for the benefit and profit of both corporations and shareholders. The present global economy has allowed rich countries to keep on reaping the benefits and resources of less fortunate countries where the wealth distribution is often concentrated into the hands of dictators and wealthy corporations, while the people of the country have virtually nothing. The result is a shrinking middle class, a national economy with very little manufacturing or value-added sectors, and low-paying service sector jobs.

We are seeing revolutions starting in countries that have been long controlled by dictators who have starved the poor while stealing all of the riches.

The world has been influenced by two different models of economy: *communism*—where people are obliged to share all they have and earn, and *capitalism*—where people keep all they have for themselves, with no obligation or responsibility to others. Neither model is working.

Currently, we are stuck with an economy that only takes from the people and doesn't consider empowering individuals, only using them to promote the interests of the rich.

What is the result of a misguided economy? People today have become completely absorbed by constant worries for the economy, losing their personal power in the thought that they will be deprived in some way in the future. They are obsessed with buying and spending to fulfill some empty sense of happiness. Their minds are constantly busy and preoccupied, allowing no time for quiet reflection or spiritual growth. Pleasure and idleness have become the misguided result.

Very few have any idea what economy really means.

Why are we in this situation? Because, in general, the economy is based on the inferior nature of human beings; hunger for profit and fear of losing are such that swindling, usury, and dishonesty have become acceptable. As long as these motives belong to the lower nature, which only wants to take, no stable or durable progress will be guaranteed because ethics and morality will be compromised to favor the said economy.

What is the solution then? Considering the economy from a higher, divine point of view may be the solution since a healthy economy cannot be run by individuals whose psychic energies are wasted on destructive thoughts and desires. It must start with a higher perspective, a spiritual perspective of equilibrium.

THE ECONOMY FROM A SPIRITUAL PERSPECTIVE

There is another aspect of the human nature, the higher Self, the divine nature. From this level, we can look at the economy for more sustainable viability. We mentioned earlier that people seek happiness through possessions and comfort but do not necessarily find it. That is because happiness, joy, love, and wisdom do not belong to the lower nature; they belong to a higher, more subtle part of our nature—our soul and spirit.

Of course, to learn and correct everything at once is not realistic, but we can at least be willing to take some steps in the direction of our deepest desires that lie at the heart of our being, beyond the mask of the superficial desires and external possessions.

When human beings decide to use all economic means in the service of their spiritual, divine nature, prosperity will follow. If all the efforts generated to become rich on the outside were transposed to becoming richer inwardly, people would blossom and swim in happiness. All the elements of life would follow a proper order, from top to bottom, rather than being simply based on the bottom (the materialistic aspect) and cut from the head (the spiritual aspect), thus avoiding so many problems and imbalances.

By concentrating on the economic side, governments are leading the world into degeneracy and decadence;

maintenance of a position of greater power and wealth over the rest of the world calls for actions that are not primarily honest, and that is fatal to civilization. When prosperity increases on the one hand and respect for the divine laws decreases on the other, the result has always been disastrous for the world.[18]

Divine laws are those governing the higher, more divine side of human beings and all of nature. An economy that is guided by the higher world puts its emphasis on the enlightenment of people, attentiveness, and helping people become careful and reasonable in its attitude to others.

It is essential for a good economy to first recognize the structure of human beings with their lower and higher natures—and their connection to the entire universe which is organized as a hierarchy. Everything human beings do must correspond to a model, a celestial idea. Then, everything—all the processes and achievements—will be perfect.

FINDING THE BALANCE

Jesus said, "Render unto Caesar the things which are Caesar's, and unto God the things that are God's." If we look at this parable a little closer, we see that Jesus was trying to give us the example of balance, of economy. Caesar represents the state, the economy, and God represents the divine side in us. They are two different aspects of life, and we must always take time for both to obtain a balance or equilibrium.

Today, we are completely absorbed by the economic side of life, and there is very little time left for the divine side. Quiet reflection and attentiveness to our energies is what is needed.

Nature is the first model for a true economy. With nature, nothing is ever lost—not a single atom. Everything is recovered

---

18   Omraam Mikhaël Aïvanhov, *Under the Dove: The Reign of Peace,* Izvor Collection #208, France, Prosveta S.A., ed. 1984, p. 95.

and reused. With human beings, on the contrary, one half works to repair the damages generated by the other half. Waste and garbage are accumulating to the point that the management of such has become a problem on the planet. So, managing the economy could at least begin with developing the attention. For example, paying attention to one's gestures when moving things in such a way so as not to hit or break them would save a lot of effort and energy!

Moreover, if developing the attention on the physical plane is a first step toward a better understanding of the economy, the second would be to consider developing attention at a higher level, such as an observation of self, and an awareness of consciousness. This process would enable us to recognize the currents and influences that move through us and then to better manage our own energies.

THE NEW ECONOMY

Giving after taking is the first principle of justice. Giving and taking are like the two pans on a pair of scales. When you take, you must give to restore balance. And even if you do not take, you must also give. Why? Because in this way you set up a motion and receive something in return. But begin at least by learning to give when you have taken; this in itself will be progress.[19]

We are seeing representations in the world today of programs that reflect the idea of a more balanced economy, an economy that gives power back to the people. *Microcredit*[20] systems in developing countries are based upon the idea of lending smaller amounts to individuals, empowering them to take it upon themselves to create work and earn a living. This is only one example of a sustainable way to help individuals get out of poverty and not depend on governments and large corporations to provide work.

---

19 Omraam Mikhaël Aïvanhov, *Daily Meditations*, France, Prosveta S.A., 2011, for March 30, 2012. p. 96.

20 http://en.wikipedia.org/wiki/Microcredit

What can we do about the economy? We can be the physical representative of a healthy economy in our own way by balancing our needs for material possessions with the development of our psychic and physical well-being.

To be really happy and healthy, one must look to the higher planes where wisdom, love, and truth reside in the realm of the soul and the spirit. One needs to find a balance between the idea of only seeking comfort and the search for the inner riches such as happiness, peace, and wisdom.

And again, we need to be attentive and present in the daily decisions we make to see whether they are leading us toward enlightenment, self-control, and helpfulness. In becoming attentive, reasonable and masters of ourselves, we practice true economy.

Exercise: Repeat the following affirmation three times to get a great sense of balance:

"I am stable,
son/daughter of the stable one,
conceived and engendered in the realm of stability."

Pair of Scales

CHAPTER 3
Education versus Pedagogy

THROUGHOUT ALL CIVILIZATIONS, IN one form or another, education has always been a fundamental element in the process of preparing individuals to face life, to act in accordance with its demands, and to give it the most appropriate mode of expression for the blossoming of people and of society in general.

In a literal sense, education is the art of giving each human being, at any time and at any age, the proper means for developing and expressing the qualities, virtues, and gifts carried within as seeds. It is, therefore, natural to think that any education or pedagogy must be based on the knowledge of human structure in the entirety of its nature and manifestations. It is evident that talking about human nature implies a vast question: what is this nature? What are the forces, visible and invisible, that influence and define it, and when?

Even if we agree with the idea that many scientific and philosophical disciplines try to find answers to this question, we are bound to notice that their findings remain incomplete and disassociated. The limitation of these approaches resides in their tendency to objectivize—an exercise that often leads to treating the consequences while omitting the causes. The inability of so-called "official sciences" to shed light and fully explain the transformation and the evolution of individuals has led many people to consider a broader, spiritual point of view of the human being. This broadened view would see a more unified and integrated way of understanding human nature and include its more subtle dimensions, such as the soul and the spirit.

This broader spiritual understanding of human beings will undoubtedly reveal a different context with a spectrum of modified needs and greater possibilities of manifestation and expression. And it is here that the true science of education begins.

First, taking into account the evolutionary principle governing human beings, the notion of reincarnation implies that they already had a past here on earth, as well as a present they must now live while improving as much as possible, and a future they are called to prepare for with each new day. In relation to education, this evolutionary cycle means that it defines the meaning of existence, particularly the quest for perfection. Thus, one of the missions of pedagogy is to contribute to the perfection of human beings.

This is where education differs from simple instruction. Today, in almost all countries, instruction defines the line of conduct regarding pedagogy. Indeed, as everyone can see in consultation with the national representatives in charge of political and pedagogical strategy, this instruction's single objective is primarily to develop the intellectual faculties and knowledge with little consideration for moral values.

By comparison, education, as described here, is for the following:

- To further encourage and cultivate the development of character (which endows a being with the right attitude to adopt in all circumstances of life).
- To surpass oneself (which contributes to strengthening the necessary willpower for any manifestation and gives hope to surpass all of one's limitations one day).
- To bring a sense of heroism (which carries a tremendous satisfaction through feeling useful to others).

As presented earlier, human beings, from a spiritual perspective, are comprised of two particular aspects or natures: the self-oriented, egocentric one referred to as the inferior nature or *personality*, and the altruistic, divine one referred to as the superior nature or *individuality*. Each having specific needs, these natures play a different role in life and in the evolution of people. If the personality is useful in its capacity to offer physical support to the life of a being, the *individuality* has the means to transform and make the expression of life more divine.

Therefore, another mission of the science of education is to pursue a fair development of people, taking into account what motivates them and helps them blossom. There are an increasing number of school dropouts in most modern countries, in part, because the programs and teachings dispensed are, in general, focused on promoting the development of the intellect of children and teenagers—and for the pure materialistic purpose of forming future contributors to economic activity. But, a human being is composed, not only of an intellect, but of a heart, willpower, a soul, and a spirit that deserve as much attention. This allows a better distribution of inner forces and, consequently, a more balanced development. Otherwise, children and youth are exposed to the danger of a premature saturation of the intellect, resulting in a lack of interest for school and learning.

The phenomenon of dropping out of school can also be explained by the fact that young people do not find true models to follow in their instructors since today's instruction does not require any moral fiber in the profession.

THE NECESSITY FOR THE EDUCATION OF PARENTS

> Within each child lies Heaven and Hell and the future development of the child depends upon those tendencies that parents will awaken and develop in him/her.[21] [Our translation]

---

21 Omraam Mikhaël Aïvanhov, *La Pédagogie Initiatique*, Oeuvres Complètes, Vol. 27, France, Prosveta S.A., 1981, p. 20.

For parents who are concerned about giving their children an education that contributes to their holistic development, the knowledge of the two aspects of human nature emphasizes the importance of studying and understanding the human inner structure. Parents must engage in a process that allows them to accomplish within themselves what is demanded of the child so they become models to follow. To be complete and applicable in all life situations, this process must evidently be spiritual. Only a broad spiritual understanding of life and the structure of human nature can bring about suitable methods for a proper undertaking of self-improvement.

> Most parents wishing an easy life of riches and success for their children are evidently doing so from love, but it is a type of love that does not consider the truest evolution for these children. Of course, I am not saying that parents should wish their children to suffer but their wish should only be that their children become benefactors of humanity and then it is up to Heaven to decide the experiences they will go through to get there.[22]
> [Our translation]

Such a belief is possible after a change in perspective; it comes from a new vision of the world, of a proper understanding of the mission of man on earth. To transform the earth into a garden of paradise is the dream that we all carry within us—except that the methods to fulfill it require each of us, particularly parents, to undertake a work of transformation and dedicate ourselves to the alchemy that will make us temples where the divine will dwell and manifest itself for the good of all.

---

22 Omraam Mikhaël Aïvanhov, *Vie et travail à l'école divine*, Oeuvres Complètes, Vol. 31, France, Prosveta S.A., éd. 1991, p. 221.

EDUCATION BEGINS BEFORE BIRTH

In describing the subtle forces and mechanisms inherent in human beings, the larger spiritual concept of galvanoplasty, which we will be discussing in the chapter on women, focuses on the process of consciously bringing children into the world from the time of conception, through the gestation period, and up to birth. For those future parents prepared to do this work, it allows an incredible opportunity to attract souls with all the virtues, qualities and gifts they wish for their children to develop.

Like the seed that carries within it the image of the tree, the father gives the mother the blueprint of the future child upon which she elaborates. We will come back later to this important question in the chapter about women and motherhood; they hold the keys to the future of their children and humanity.

EDUCATION AND THE FUTURE OF HUMANITY

The question of education concerns all of us because we are parents and educators of our own thoughts and feelings. They are our first children and our most important responsibility. By watching over our thoughts and feelings, we become true models for our family. It is through the transformation and improvement of every one of us that the whole of humanity will progress toward perfection and the realization of an age where we all will recognize each other as brothers and sisters, sons and daughters of the same Celestial Father and the same Divine Mother: the Golden Age of the poets.

Humans also are that kind of ferment, or leaven. If we are ferment in the spiritual sense, then, simply by coming in contact with others, by our presence alone, we can influence mankind, it all depends on the intensity of our light, the intensity of our love, the intense force that comes from the life we live! To acquire that intensity, we need a Teaching, a system, methods. Once you have gained a new understanding and give it the food of intense love, the only thing left to change is your life. A new intense life! Everything becomes easy, everything is harmonious, because you yourself are a beneficent factor, a good influence on all mankind.[23]

Exercise: For a few moments, let us concentrate and imagine that the earth and all its inhabitants are wrapped in an intense luminous light, which, little by little, penetrates all human beings and layers of the earth, transforming and illuminating everything in its path.

At the end, the earth appears like an immense round crystal through which rays of luminous beams sparkle. The creatures on this new earth now shine and radiate like little suns being born in a new galaxy.

Terre de cristal © Louiselle www.jardinsdecristal.com

---

23 Omraam Mikhaël Aïvanhov, *Aquarius, Herald of the Golden Age*, Complete Works, Vol. 26, France, Prosveta S.A., ed. 1981, pp. 146-147.

CHAPTER 4
Evolution and Involution

IT IS NOT POSSIBLE to talk about evolution without taking into consideration the law of hierarchy. Starting with the kingdoms, one realizes the degree of vitality is what defines these kingdoms best. For example, this is easy to understand beginning with the mineral kingdom where inertia is most evident, then progressing to the vegetable kingdom where the movement begins to manifest itself, then the animal kingdom where the expression is more lively and interactive and, finally, the human kingdom where intelligence blossoms. But who says that it terminates at this level? Why should it not continue with the more subtle kingdoms: from angels to archangels all to way to the throne of God?

At one point or other in life, one asks where do we come from and why do we live? These are fundamental questions of existence. Be it by questioning, great suffering, or simply through intuition, nearly all of us have asked those questions. Where do we come from? Where do we go from here? What is the meaning of life? Many have termed this phase "the existential crisis."

For some, these questions were the beginning of a personal quest that led them on the path of self-development, while others, blinded by circumstances, continue like automatons without trying to find a satisfying answer or simply repress those questions. Whether we find an answer or not, we continue to go on living as if there is an unconscious force pushing us forward. The difference lies in the awareness of consciousness.

If we accept hierarchy in the kingdoms and in the evolution of beings, it also means that we each find ourselves somewhere within this great evolutionary chain, and, that step by step, we grow toward our own perfection until one day we too shall become as perfect as our Creator.

This evolution is not simply a question of reasoning. It is a learning acquired through experience into matter. Knowledge becomes flesh and bone. We create links to free ourselves from them until we reach an absolute freedom. And for this to take place, it is necessary for us to go through the involution phase: descending into matter in order to know it better, to master it, and to elevate ourselves above it. Our thoughts create, our emotions mold, and our acts bear reactions or consequences. In order to become perfect co-creators, it is necessary to modify the imperfections of our creations here on earth; this will take time.

When we accept reincarnation, we accept the full responsibility of our own evolution. We can no longer blame our parents, society, or even religion for our life circumstances as they are a consequence of our own behavior on all levels—physical, emotional, intellectual, and spiritual. Reincarnation is based on the law of action and reaction. It is one of the fundamental cosmic laws: one reaps what one sows, and this law acts on all levels of existence, beyond time and space. By accepting reincarnation, we find the key that shapes our future. We become the masters of our own destiny.

Reincarnation is mentioned in most of the sacred texts and even in the Gospels. If we knew how to read the meaning of the texts, we would find several passages referring to it. Master Aïvanhov demonstrates it clearly in one of his lectures from the pocket book collection entitled *Man, Master of his Destiny* in the chapter dedicated to reincarnation. Moreover, reincarnation was common knowledge among Christians until the fourth century when it was decreed by the Council of Nicaea that all references to reincarnation be removed so that the Church would be the supreme authority to judge people and thereby allow access to God.

At present, the majority of human beings are relatively well educated, and they measure the degree of their advancement on their intellectual knowledge, their position in society, or their riches. In general, this form of intelligence is so entrenched in the idea of gain, motivated by personal interests and the exploitation of nature, and even of human beings, that the name "materialist" is totally fitting to that behavior. Of course, this same form of intelligence, and all the inventions related to it, has the purpose of making life easier. However, in reality, people feel that, despite all this progress and the modern inventions, their lives have become increasingly complicated.

Moreover, there is a great deal of suffering related to stress and anxiety, even among the youth of today. In the past, several civilizations vanished. At present, as the intellect dominates with its cunning, injustices, and abuses, it puts humanity at risk—unless a better balance is achieved in human behavior by developing the qualities of the heart, goodness, and a spirit of cooperation and fraternity.

During the course of this materialization and descent into matter, we identify ourselves so much with matter, and even with the physical body, that we no longer recognize the subtle aspects of our being. We are alive and active, but do we know the intense life? Intense life, not in the sense of passions but of the subtle life, the life of the soul and the spirit, where true happiness, joy, unconditional love, intelligence of the heart, and intuition reside. Our identification with matter is at the cost of our inner development and the discovery of riches buried deep within ourselves that only await the right moment to emerge.

Master Omraam Mikhaël Aïvanhov relates the following story in one of his lectures:

> One day an Angel decided to come down to earth to study the life of humans and animals. To materialize, he took the form of a pig. Life was wonderful, he ate acorns and a certain mixture ... what do you call it ... Oh yes! pâté. And he was

immensely happy. He took a wife and was soon surrounded by numerous little piglets. My God, what bliss! Never would he leave such bliss. Above, his fellow-angels waited, heads bowed, wondering how to make him return. They sent message after message, but as far as he was concerned, life was perfect, he was in clover! In the end, they decided the only solution would be to have him killed and cooked for dinner. When the angel came out of his appetizing form, he was horrified at having been content as an animal and he thanked his fellow angels for delivering him![24]

We resemble somewhat the angel in this anecdote, having descended into matter to the point that we have forgotten our roots, our true identity. We must learn anew who we are, going through the evolutionary hierarchy in order to improve and reintegrate the lost paradise of the soul and the spirit. To achieve this, we change "clothing" from one incarnation to the next.

All the cosmos is in evolution, and our solar system is also moving in precise, evolutionary cycles. We are presently terminating the Piscean Era and are entering the Aquarian Era. The Piscean Age is the symbol of sacrifice and the culminating point of our descent into matter. In this Aquarian Age, our consciousness must wake up to the acceptance of the life of the soul and the spirit so that we learn to "know thyself." This knowledge of our true Self will reveal the secrets of the universe that the great Masters and Initiates of all the ages have revealed to their disciples.

Let us come back, for one moment, to these two processes of involution and evolution. To better illustrate these two movements and the interdependence connecting them, let us take the example of the desire to build a house. First, one needs to work on ideas and draw a plan. This represents involution: the descent of ideas onto paper. Then the construction begins on the physical plane:

---

24 Omraam Mikhaël Aïvanhov, *Aquarius, Herald of the Golden Age,* Complete Works, vol. 26, France, Prosveta S.A., ed. 1981 p. 17.

the foundation, the structure, the roof, and lastly the inside décor. Finally, human beings come to dwell in it. That represents the evolutionary movement: going from the most material to the more subtle.

It is the same process when we decide to work on ourselves, on our inner life. We must begin with the involution movement—that which is most subtle, the world of ideas in the causal plane—in order to make those ideas descend into a visible, concrete manifestation. Then, the development of those ideas in the physical plane, until the idea reaches perfection, represents the movement of evolution.

Our development follows the same processes. We come down into matter; this is the involution movement, and now we must complete our evolution by turning toward the knowledge of our inner realm. To do this, we need to invite the spirit to dwell, or descend, into our physical body to make it more luminous, more alive, until it becomes as one with it. For the spirit, it is the movement of involution; for us, it is a movement of evolution. Until now, these two movements have remained separate for the majority of people except for the great Sages and Masters who know how to marry the two movements to live within the unity of their own being.

One can also understand the relationship between involution and evolution through breathing where the movements of inhalation and exhalation complement each other, allowing the circulation of air in and out of the body to promote health. Each has its own specific function but is dependent on the other to benefit the whole.

Thus, we are part of a very well-orchestrated, harmonious system which, despite appearances, assures the whole of our evolution.

Master Aïvanhov explains the following:

> True creation is not something stagnant, it is not a mere reproduction, a copy; it is one step forward, an evolution. It is thanks to this creative instinct that individuals and the cosmos as a whole evolve. With

the single exception of God himself, everything has to evolve.[25]

The missing key at present in our evolution is the conscious participation of spirit—the awareness of consciousness of oneself as spirit, omnipotent, omniscient, and omnipresent. Spirit in its movement of involution through our consciousness can vivify our matter, our body, and all our manifestations. It makes our existence pure, transparent, harmonious, balanced, healthy, and safe!

Spirit always seeks its involution through our consciousness while we are pursuing our evolution. Presently, on planet Earth, evolution left in the hands of the ego and of fanatical religious groups, does not serve the glorious future of humanity. On the contrary, the current conditions have become so powerful that we are on the brink of auto-destruction. Human beings must wake up and find a way to remedy the abuses on all levels unless Cosmic Intelligence plays its part and brings a better balance.

Moreover, the cycles of involution—our descent into matter, and of evolution—our consciousness reaching its divine bliss, are in fact only small cycles of the greater evolutionary cycles of our planet and beyond, of our galaxy, and of the whole cosmos. Science today easily explains the cycles of day and night and of the seasons through the position of the earth and the rotation of its axis. Some scientists have been studying the extrapolation of these cycles by suggesting that the earth goes through certain very precise cycles, like those of day and night but on a much larger scale involving thousands of years, and noticed these movements of involution and evolution. The writings of Gregg Braden on the subject of cycles are most informative.

It is interesting to note that, when difficulties arise, everyone is ready to make efforts to improve their situations. The need to survive opens up new channels of receptivity and helps develop undreamed of virtues and qualities. In normal circumstances, a level of complacency dominates but, when challenges arise, a wakeup call brings a level of awareness, prompting one to surpass oneself. Sometimes, it feels

---

25   Omraam Mikhaël Aïvanhov, *Cosmic Moral Laws,* Complete Works, Vol. 12, France, Prosveta S.A. ed. 1989, p. 63.

as if we need obstacles to wake us up and, like ants, we keep going forward until we encounter a wall and then we change direction … fortunately. On the other hand, there are many people who are becoming awakened—thanks to inner development, to their intuition, or because they have had the blessing of being stimulated by the truths of a spiritual Master. These beings, today, move silently toward a new life and, through their behavior, their emanations influence all those around them.

We are most privileged to live in the present age. It feels as if we are experiencing many incarnations in one. We also have the opportunity to transform ourselves at incredible speeds. In the past, those beings who wanted to grow spiritually had to undergo trials for several years before being accepted in the school of an Initiate. The knowledge of the Sages was only revealed once the disciples had proven their fidelity. Moreover, they were subjected to demanding initiations to test their physical, mental, and spiritual capacities. Today, initiations are found in daily life. Knowledge is easily accessible to everyone without fear or danger of an inquisition. The avenues are wide open for discovery, exploration, and the integration of the great truths that lead to the inner world. All one needs is the good will to feel that there is more to life than merely seeking material riches and the sincere desire to know oneself. The awakening in consciousness is a personal responsibility; when this awakening takes place on a global scale, all the elements of life will be transformed, bringing harmony and balance to the individual and all nations. The respect for one another and toward Mother Earth will become sacrosanct.

Perhaps you have heard of the theory of the one hundred monkeys? It is based on morphic resonance and explains how a young monkey on a Japanese island began washing his potatoes before eating them and how, after a certain time, others started imitating him. When it came to the ninety-ninth monkey, an interesting phenomenon happened: just one more monkey and, all of a sudden, the entire community began washing their potatoes. Furthermore, in a short while, the monkeys from the nearby islands all began washing their potatoes as well. The application of this theory means that if there are a sufficient number of beings who begin working on themselves, awakening their consciousness to the divine world and increasing their degree of luminosity, a flip in the entire consciousness of human beings will take place and humanity will wake up to its divinity. Perhaps we represent the one hundredth monkey? Why not? We would be the first ones to benefit from it on an individual level, then on a community level, and, finally, on the planetary level!

Exercise: In order to feel the unity with all of life, we invite you to visualize that you are a luminous point and that this point grows to include all of your being, the space where you are, the city or country where you live, the whole planet, and even beyond: spreading the light into the solar system, the stars, the galaxy, and finally the entire universe. Feel that you are vibrating in unison with the evolution of all this cosmic life. Allow yourself to be rocked by these wonderful energies that participate in your blossoming.

Inner Flame © Julia Byrne

CHAPTER 5
The Role of Women and Motherhood

The Two Principles

For many centuries, women have been despised by religion, society, or the dominant patriarchal model. Nowadays, in many developed countries, women have acquired, through great efforts and sacrifices, their own independence and recognition. Yet, in numerous other cultures, women are still in last place: neglected, rejected, abused, burned, or drowned.

It is of primary importance to give women their proper place and to understand their role in society and their true value to humanity at large.

The universe stems from the world of principles (about which we will explain more in the chapter on Nature). The world of principles and laws govern us, whether we are conscious of it or not, as they are the foundation that assures harmony and the circulation of life in every domain of existence—from the invisible to the visible world.

These manifestations are innumerable and diverse everywhere in nature.

At the root of life, the masculine and feminine principles are inseparable and indispensable for any form of creation. They both have very determined functions, but one is as important as the other—like opposite poles allowing life to circulate.

Take the example of yin and yang. Each part plays its role and accepts the other in perfect harmony. Look at electricity and magnetism: when an imbalance occurs within the atmosphere, nature remedies that imbalance through storm or rain.

It is the same for humanity: as principles, men and women create life, assuring the continuation of the species. Throughout our incarnations, we have the possibility of experimenting with both roles. Moreover, if we are born as a man or a woman, it is because the soul has chosen that experience to reach a better balance between the two principles and to pursue its evolution.

When only the masculine principle dominates, an imbalance takes place on a personal or social scale. Today, for example, in some cultures, the birth of boys is privileged to the detriment of girls up to the point of eliminating the female fetus. Thus, a demographic imbalance is created within one generation, often resulting in violence, abuse, and intolerable behavior.

Nature knows how to find its balance but, with human beings, disharmony is brought on by the abuse of power or sheer ignorance. If only an equivalent importance was given to both principles, such an imbalance would not exist.

The role of the masculine principle, of man, is to create—to carry the seed. Men are emissive. They engender. They represent the yin or "electric" aspect. On the other hand, the role of the feminine principle, of woman, is to form. Women are receptive. They receive the seed, attract and contain the elements for the formation of a being to eventually be born. They represents the yang or "magnetic" aspect. The feminine and masculine principles become indispensable collaborators in an equal and inseparable manner.

Men and women are equal to each other in their own domains. In the physical plane, man is superior by his strength. In the astral plane, where the emotions and feelings dominate, women are emissive and all powerful. Women are the source of inspiration for men; women influence men to make the best possible decisions.

The ideal for each is to develop aspects of both principles in order to find a better balance within themselves and their interactions with others.

FINDING A SOUL MATE

All beings dream of finding their soul mate, but the Initiatic Tradition tells us that is rather rare. In fact, it will only happen twelve times throughout our entire evolution! It is a dream that many young people cherish and, in their hurry to find it, tend to be led astray too often. One needs to be patient and develop the criteria to be able to choose a partner wisely.

Infatuation is not a good option when considering love; it is best to seek harmony within first on the physical, emotional, and intellectual levels. Physical attraction is not enough because, when problems arise, attraction alone will not solve them. Also, there must be an affinity, both emotionally and intellectually. If one can agree with each other's tastes, desires, and ideas, this will lead to better understanding and harmony. Sometimes, a couple may not feel any actual physical attraction, but they will feel the love. This is because there is much to share and they feel very close to each other. It is most important to share the same ideals and goals and to have an intimate communion of the mind. When the soul and the spirit are in primary place, they bring light and nobility to love.

> In the new Teaching [...] instead of loving only a man or woman's personality, their physical body, you love their Spirit, their soul, the Source, God. That love will last forever, even when you are old [...] because it was not the physical body you fell in love with, it was the being, the divine reflection of God Himself.[26]

For true love to exist, each person must be exemplary in sincerity and honesty; it is the foundation needed for a lasting relationship. Nothing is nobler or more luminous than the meeting of a man and woman who are consciously aware of their responsibility to this truth.

---

26 Omraam Mikhaël Aïvanhov, *The Key to Solve the Problem of Existence.* Complete Works, Vol. 11, France, Prosveta S.A., ed. 2003, p. 214.

The best way to find one's soul mate is firstly to harmonize the feminine and masculine principles within oneself. This work will generate all necessary emanations and radiations to attract a being with the same aspirations.

Beauty: An Essential Element for Women

Everyone is attracted by beauty; women, by virtue of their nature on earth, are the guardians of beauty and harmony. They transmit and maintain the ideal of beauty in matter. They have a duty to maintain and transmit it to their children.

Nature has given women vanity. It has also inspired them to become more beautiful themselves and to transmit this to their children in order to make humanity more beautiful as well. Vanity can also become their greatest downfall should they use it to manipulate men. Too often, women abuse men with their gestures, words, or attitudes. And men fall for it! Too often, deceptions and false pretense have been used to achieve their aims.

The challenge of the work with beauty is to know its purpose and the way to use it. Instead of using it to seduce and to satisfy one's vanity, it would be wiser if women used it to grow and blossom, and become an example, a model to inspire other women and young girls. They would learn to nourish and develop a great ideal. Knowing how to use their beauty, women can influence a whole nation to follow her lead.

Imagine a being who seriously adopts a sublime idea, a great ideal; little by little, this new philosophy impregnates all the cells. The very matter of the physical body changes from the inside out. That being becomes lovelier, even if it takes years for the body to become the reflection of the beauty of their soul and spirit. Inversely, a person who is outwardly gorgeous, but who leads a life of debauchery, will not lose her or his appearance immediately, but one day, the inner ugliness will take over the face, gestures, etc. It is only a matter of time!

Women have always been linked closely to beauty; unfortunately, in their haste to adopt plastic surgery or artificial enhancements, they often lose the essence of inner beauty and become superficial and insignificant in this pursuit. To seek to improve one's face or body is simply working on the surface. This will only result in a short-term solution; working on one's inner beauty is slower, but it lasts much longer.

There is a considerable difference between exterior appearance and interior beauty. How to find a solution? Matter changes more slowly than one's thoughts or feelings do. One can easily change one's mind and direction—or adopt a new philosophy for a more elevated ideal—but the face remains the same for many years. True beauty is not in its form but in its radiations and emanations; it is the quintessence of the soul. It is the reflection of one's inner garden. It is the psychic life that takes expression in an external appearance—and not the opposite. In nourishing the soul and the heart with sublime feelings filled with love, we water the flowers of our inner garden. This beauty will seek to take expression, manifest, and reflect itself on the physical appearance.

> The face you have today was once the face your soul had in another life. It is the net result of all the virtues and vices you have cultivated in the past, and if you do not like it, there is not much you can do to change it now. So, instead of bothering about your physical face, you would do much better to take care of that other face which is the original, the inner model which has determined the form of your physical face. [...] The face of the soul is very powerful and it imposes its features on the physical face.[27]

WOMEN IN THEIR ROLE AS EDUCATORS

The union of man and woman is the first institution on earth: humanity, through the ages, exists from this union! History is woven with the threads of centuries of these alliances, fusions, and

---

27 Omraam Mikhaël Aïvanhov, *Creation Artistic and Spiritual*, Izvor #223, France, Prosveta S.A., ed. 1988, p. 131.

intimacies—whether they were proper or not. And everyone bears the mark; each human being is a reflection of the quality of the union between the father and the mother!

Did you know that—even before conception—the parents play a determining role in the quality of being they will attract to the family? The child can be very ordinary or very extraordinary!

The seed the father gives resembles him: everything he has lived, every thought, feeling, and action he has expressed is found in his seed. He is the progenitor—in the image of the tree and the seed. The role of the mother is to take the seed, to model it, and to bring it to fruition. It is the most important event on earth! How can it be left to coincidental meeting, to a state of being more or less conscious, when bringing a new soul to earth is surely the most glorious opportunity for a man and a woman? It is a precious and crucial moment when both presence of mind and state of their souls can overcome physical and psychic limitations.

It is thanks to a woman's magnetism that she is all powerful in this formative role. Whether she is aware of it or not, nature gives her the gift of being able to attract all the necessary elements to form and materialize the life in her womb. Most women have no idea of the tremendous influence they exercise on the child they bear.

Everything a woman thinks, feels, and lives emotionally is transferred to the fetus during the gestation period. It is both extraordinary and troubling because, according to the state of mind of the mother, the child will be of the same quality, of the same essence. She has great powers during the gestation period: nine months of intense preparation for the entire life of her child and the decades of manifestations that will follow! Through her thoughts and feelings, she acts on her child like the process of electroplating: the process of depositing, through electrolysis, a layer of gold on a metal to cover it. This same process that applies to the mother was referred to by Master Aïvanhov in his lectures as Spiritual Galvanoplasty.[28] He states that women could transform humanity in less than a generation through this conscious process.

---

28 See the chapter on Spiritual Galvanoplasty in the Izvor #203; *Education begins before birth.*

If the thoughts and the feelings are pure and luminous throughout the formative state, the nature of the child will be noble, generous, and incorruptible. In all the circumstances of life, that being will be able to sustain a good direction and purpose.

Moreover, if the mother eats nutritious food and nourishes herself with beautiful colors and music—and if she links with the beauty of nature and surrounds herself with splendid colors, asking the help of the luminous spirits—she will attract golden particles to make her child nobler. With this incredible power, she can model, transform, and better define the character of her children.

> Now you see why it is so vitally important for a pregnant woman to harbor only luminous thoughts. Thanks to her thoughts, the seed that is growing within her will absorb the pure, precious materials she gives it and, one day, she will bring into the world a great artist or a brilliant scientist, a saint, a messenger from God. A mother can accomplish great miracles because she holds the key to the forces of life. [...] Once a child is born, she cannot have such an influence ... the nature of the child is already determined![29]

Women, in their role as mothers, are primarily educators, ideal pedagogues for the future of their children but also as educators of men by educating their sons. Women have the responsibility to inspire men through their thoughts, feelings, and actions—and they can help men accomplish the most noble of deeds. Did you know that deep down inside, men only want to be uplifted and inspired by women?

---

29 Omraam Mikhaël Aïvanhov, *Education begins before birth*, Izvor #203, France, Prosveta S.A., 1986, p. 29.

THE POWER OF THE WOMEN COLLECTIVE

The formative power that women are gifted with can be used not only to improve the quality of beings incarnating on earth—but also on the psychic plane to help the formation and manifestation of a sublime, noble idea, as in the case of the seed for the child.

For men, it is essential to discover their inner woman, which is their imagination, in order to be able to participate in this great collective work. To develop their inner woman, men must allow the manifestation of the qualities of goodness, tenderness, and humility. They must become like the pregnant woman: receptive, dedicated, protective, and discreet—qualities that are essentially feminine. In fact, each thought is just as important as the creation of a child. Each thought becomes, one day, a realization.

And if a Sage or an Initiate were to bring a sublime idea, the seed of the Golden Age, and if all women on earth decided to gather in thought to offer their formative energies, this idea would be birthed in a relatively short time.

There is a saying which goes as: "What women want, God wants." Most assuredly this popular adage indicates the magical power that women hold. Women have the power to materialize things. Even if women are single, all women are mothers of their thoughts and their feelings. They possess an intellect and a heart that radiates and emanates, and they all can form a "symbolic" child. Moreover, it is a thousand times more important because this child is formed collectively for the well-being of humanity.

If all women on earth decided to unite with their thoughts on the psychic level to help the formation of a new idea, such as a new kingdom, a garden of peace, and love, a new era would be born on earth—and it would be the Golden Age. Women have the power and the possibility because they hold the key to this formative force—the greatest gift given to women.

Exercise: Imagine that we all represent a pregnant woman and that she carries the whole planet in her womb. She carries a new earth filled with light, peace, harmony, and love. She is birthing the Golden Age on earth.

Plenitud de la Vida © Dora www.doragil.com

—————— **CHAPTER 6** ——————

Science, Conscience, and Superconsciousness

*"No problem can be solved from the same level
of consciousness that created it."*
—Albert Einstein

CONSCIOUSNESS IS A VAST subject—far too big to go into detail in this chapter alone. Many books have already examined this subject, and many more will be written in the future. The goal at present is to consider the essential elements and gain a better understanding of our own consciousness. We can learn how to use it in a practical manner to help us become more conscious, to see what is happening in our everyday lives, to create a reality more in line with our true potential, thought by thought, moment by moment, and to become the master of our own destiny.

In order to proceed, let us first establish from which perspective we will study the subject. Traditional science believes that consciousness is a byproduct of matter or is made from physical molecules moving around. Some leading-edge scientists, however, are now questioning this and rightfully so. We shall attempt to adopt the point of view from which *initiatic science* speaks as it comes from superconsciousness, which we will discuss later in this chapter.

SCIENCE

Before tackling the subject of consciousness, let us begin by the definition of the word *science,* which comes from the Latin *scientia.* According to the Webster's New Collegiate Dictionary, the definition of science is the "knowledge attained through study or practice" or "knowledge covering general truths of the operation of general laws, especially as obtained and tested through scientific method [and] concerned with the physical world."

In general, science is the result of the development of the intellect; its function is to analyze, measure, weigh, and identify elements under its scrutiny.

There is a vast array of sciences—too many to detail here—but we will focus on the science of the Initiates, named *initiatic science* by Omraam Mikhaël Aïvanhov. This science is based on the knowledge of the principles that govern our universe and of the laws and manifestations resulting from them. Great Masters and Initiates all agree on the truths revealed by this science, although they have expressed it differently through the ages. This science is acquired through sane and harmonious development on all levels: the development of consciousness, the mastery of subconscious forces, the knowledge of subtle bodies, and the blossoming of superconsciousness.

Initiatic science is not separated from the official sciences. In fact, what traditional sciences discover is often what *initiatic science* has already revealed. Let us consider one example: the science of mathematics. Initiates know that all of creation is based on the science of numbers. Indeed, the entire universe is simply composed of numbers. They recognize that numbers are pure principles that manifest and materialize in nature as mountains, rivers, crystals, metals, animals, and even human beings.

The only sciences Initiates do not recommend studying are the occult sciences because they stem from a mixture of good and bad, floundering in the dark regions where people are not sufficiently developed to control the forces they invoke in themselves, in others, or in nature. Some people explore those sciences in order to develop their personal powers, feed vanity or pride, and dominate or influence others. The Initiates only teach *initiatic science*, the spiritual science, because their goal is solely to help human beings toward perfection by showing them how to develop their superconsciousness (so they, in turn, can help humankind).

Consciousness and its Origin

What is consciousness, and where does is come from? Consciousness could be defined as a state of constant and perpetual growth into "knowledge." As conscious beings, we always are in a state of evolution, of becoming more. Consciousness is, in essence, a vibrational energy resulting from creation—with love at its very root. Its primary function is to keep expanding and evolving without ceasing. Consciousness does not remain stagnant; it keeps growing, at whatever cost, throughout the many incarnations.

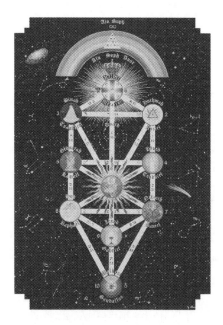

Tree of Life © Ivano Marchesani

The Cabbalah is probably one of the few teachings that give us an indication of the origin of consciousness. When we look at the image of the Tree of Life, we notice, at the top of the tree, the words *Ain Soph Aur* or "Limitless Light" and, above, we see written *Ain Soph*, which means limitless or without limit. If light represents the highest vibration in our physical universe, on the more subtle level, love is the highest vibrational energy at the heart or core of creation. *Ain Soph Aur* could thus be interpreted as "created from Unconditional Love."

It is easy to assume that consciousness is linked to the intellect, and it is in a way—yet not entirely. The intellect is this faculty, which looks at things mostly from the outside. The intellect projects a light on the consciousness, but consciousness is far more than the intellect alone. Consciousness exists as a perception—both on the outside and on the inside. As far as inner perception, it is like an eye, an awareness, which discretely, imperceptibly, observes and sometimes manifests as a warning, a premonition, prescience, or intuition (from the superconsciousness, which we will talk about further on). It is the inner self that seeks to manifest through the intelligence of a being. This inner self has the ability to merge with the entire cosmos, to enter into communication with the superior, divine world.

The function of the intellect is to project a light on objects or the element under its observation. This light should stimulate us and warm our hearts to the point that our willpower is set in motion to attempt to discover the original cause of our existence: to find God, merge into its infinity, and become ourselves the God that we have been created to become. It is through the superconsciousness that we will succeed and not by the intellect. The intellect is the stimulating element to seek to know.

According to the initiatic teaching, there are several levels of consciousness: the earth has a consciousness, as do the trees, animals, and human beings. In reality, everything is constituted of consciousness. Consciousness is a vibrational energy, a frequency, made of several levels of intensity. As an analogy, let us use electricity. It comes from a power plant at some 110,000 volts (or higher) and, with the use of transformers, comes to our homes at 110–240 volts. The same is true of consciousness: at its source, it is expressed at an immeasurable vibrational level before it manifests in the physical universe.

René Descartes (March 31, 1596–February 11, 1650), a French philosopher and writer, was dubbed the "Father of Modern Philosophy." Descartes was a major figure in the seventeenth century and is perhaps best known for the philosophical statement *Cogito ergo sum* or *I think, therefore I am.*[30] Who is this *I*, this *I am* that tries to define itself?

---

30 Desmond Clarke, *Descartes: A Biography*, Cambridge U. Press, pp. 58–59.

When we become aware of this subtlety within, we can say we are awakening. Then the *I am* grows and expands, reaching beyond the limited self and life in general to include other people's situation and help them better. Furthermore, when it begins to vibrate with everything around, harmonizing with the cosmic life, it becomes the *I am that I am*, Son of God, vast and universal. It is a question of vibration, of frequency; it is what is called a work of self-development.

As consciousness is a vibrational energy, it is based on the fundamental universal law called the law of vibration. This law stipulates that all things attract elements of the same nature; in other words by our thoughts, we determine a certain vibratory level, or "point of attraction," the equivalent of the vibrations we emit. Based on this law of vibration, we create our own reality and are the captain of our own ship or destiny. There is only one stream, one source of conscious energy, of unconditional love. But, in order for consciousness to eternally expand and to express itself in infinite ways, it requires some resistance or friction because, without it, there is no expansion. Without an opposing force, a polarization, the universe and creation would simply stop expanding. This contrast is sometimes referred to as good and evil, the plus and minus or the yin and yang.

This does not mean that there are two separates currents: good and evil. No, there is only one source or stream: good. A spring, high in the mountains, at its source is only one stream of water flowing. We can interpret this by saying that, as conscious vibrational beings, we are an integral part of this one stream. Since consciousness has been given the unconditional freedom to choose, we can either vibrate in alignment with this unconditional stream of love or resist it. Once our little spring becomes a river, we can flow downstream with it—or we can try to go upstream. In our efforts to go upstream, we will feel a certain amount of resistance, depending on how fast the river flows. In the same way, resistance can be found at all levels of creation and, from the Cabbalistic view, it goes all the way back to *Ain Soph Aur*. Of course, the resistance in our physical universe can come in many forms, colors, and flavors. We have expressed this in many ways through our bodies as they are the final result of manifested resistance.

For those who read this and feel it at the core of their being, they will also understand that, in order for world peace to exist on Earth, everyone, individually, has to first be at peace within and in alignment with one's inner being or soul. As noble as it is to pray for world peace, if the majority of human beings are not at peace with themselves, nothing will change. It would be far better to pray for mankind to first find inner peace on an individual level. Once this is accomplished, world peace will result because it is decreed by the law of vibration. In our alignment with our inner being, the spirit of true life will flow through our bodies—and we will receive true comprehension. A profound comprehension also brings a feeling of intense joy and expanded consciousness.

CONSCIOUSNESS AND SUB-CONSCIOUSNESS

There are many levels of consciousness: consciousness itself, unconsciousness, sub-consciousness, self-consciousness, and superconsciousness. To better explain all of these levels of consciousness, let us take the following example: if a man faints, we say he is unconscious—he does not know what is happening around him. When he begins to move about, he enters the level of the sub-conscious, like moving during sleep, and then he awakens and regains consciousness. When he comes to his senses and begins to talk, we say he is self-conscious. Now, with the sensation of being alive, happy, and feeling hope, he is filled with gratitude toward heaven; this state of consciousness is the superconsciousness.

Consciousness is not limited to brain activity. It is the total sum of the consciousness of each of the cells in the body. Our physical body is made of approximately forty-five trillion cells; each cell has its own unique consciousness and experiences during its lifetime. The consciousness of each and every cell and the consciousness of the body are so intertwined that there is no defined line between them; it is like the rainbow where it is impossible to say precisely where one color stops and the next begins.

It was first thought that genes and DNA determined our biology, but leading-edge scientists such as Dr. Rupert Sheldrake, Dr. Bruce Lipton, and others are laying the foundation of the new science of Epigenetics. They agree that the DNA is not based just on history of the genes but also controlled by signals from outside the cell, from its environment. This includes the energetic messages emanating from our positive and negative thoughts. This concept has been taught by the pedagogue and Sage, Omraam Mikhaël Aïvanhov, who has been suggesting this idea since the late 1930s.

The subconscious is like a tape that records all of our programming. It holds the imprint of everything that has been recorded by us—not only since birth, but from the point of conception as an embryo and during the nine months of gestation. One could even go further back and include the conscious state of the couple at the time of co-creation. So, from conception, our subconscious is formed and starts to record and imprint everything on the cells, forming the fetus and beyond birth to the age of seven. Those imprints will form the basis or the foundation of the behavior patterns we will hold for most of our lives. The programming continues on a smaller scale until the age of fourteen and will be fully formed by the age of twenty-one. Of course, the programming actually never stops; it continues for as long as we live.

During our daily lives, it is this subconscious "tape" that is running most of the time and affecting how we behave and interact in daily activities. We actually input very little consciously in our daily thinking. Have you ever found yourself consciously "waking up" while driving, not remembering where your mind was for the last fifteen or twenty minutes? Who was actually driving the car? It was your subconscious doing the work. Before retiring to bed at night, if we were to reflect back on the day, we would see how little was actually done consciously—the awareness was absent.

One cannot really expand on the awakening of consciousness without giving due consideration to the power of the subconscious because they are linked together like night and day. During the day, we keep busy with occupations of all kinds and move about easily; it is a process of manifestation, but it is thanks to the night that the phase of recovery takes place. Indeed, we become recharged as the muscular, circulatory, respiratory, and nervous systems are cleansed. After a good night's sleep, we are ready for the manifestation of the coming day. The work done at the subconscious level is vital for us. It is in darkness that the light regains its full power! We can do very conscious work with the subconscious when we draw strength from it to support our spiritual development:

> The solar plexus is the seat of the subconscious, whereas consciousness resides in the brain. The subconscious is closely linked to the whole cosmos, to immensity; it represents the collective aspect of our being. When we work on this level, therefore, we are tuning in to life, immersing ourselves in the ocean of universal life; the solar plexus is our point of contact with the life of the universe, the channel through which we renew and strengthen our bonds with it, through which we vibrate in rhythm with immensity. When you want to be a free, isolated individual again, you have to move back to the level of the brain, for the property of the brain is to accentuate individuality, whereas the solar plexus restores us to the collectivity. The work of the solar plexus is a night work.[31]

One could say that consciousness is linked to the sun because it brings light, the sub-consciousness is linked to the moon with its waxing and waning phases (with which profound work can be achieved), and superconsciousness is linked to the entire cosmos.

---

31   Omraam Mikhaël Aïvanhov, *The Splendour of Tiphareth*, Complete Works, Vol. 10, France, Prosveta S.A. ed. 1987, pp. 187–188.

Consciousness and Superconsciousness

Consciousness is like a small part of the larger part that is the superconsciousness. The perception that we identify ourselves with, the *I am,* sprang forth as a thought projected from our superconsciousness onto the screen of our awareness of consciousness.

Contemporary science agreed a long time ago that we only use a small fraction of our full potential. What is this full potential they are referring to? It is certainly not the capacity for more brain power. It is said that Einstein developed his capacity to 10 percent; if that is the case, most of us are well below that. Imagine what we could achieve if we developed our capacity to its full potential—to 100 percent. According to the point of view of *initiatic science*, this full potential comes from the superconsciousness, from this inner being, this inner spark, this profound spring, our Higher Self, where everything comes from. This source is often referred to as the fountain of youth or the philosopher's stone. Superconsciousness is, in fact, the Second Birth, Self-realization, the Christ consciousness!

Superconsciousness does not emerge from the intellect but manifests through other faculties that are more subtle and sensitive, such as the intuition that lives in the soul and spirit. Our full potential is the superconsciousness; it is, in fact, the Christ within!

Master Aïvanhov teaches us the following:

> Unconsciousness corresponds to the mineral kingdom, the subconscious corresponds to the vegetable kingdom, consciousness belongs to the animal kingdom, self-consciousness belongs to the domain of human beings and superconsciousness to the domain of the Angels, which is also the domain of Masters, Initiates and supermen.[32]

It is through the superconsciousness that we can capture the celestial currents, the ideas projected by the great Masters and

---

32 Omraam Mikhaël Aïvanhov, *The Second Birth: love, wisdom and truth,* Complete works, Vol. 1, France, Prosveta S.A. ed. 1988, p. 85.

Initiates who, from a mystical center on Earth, project their light and wish happiness for all human beings.

Moreover, when our hearts are full to the brim, when we feel a great love without reason, without cause, coming from nowhere, it is because we are tapping into the higher frequencies, into the degrees of universal love. This quality of love leaves us feeling refreshed, with a purity as though we had emerged from physical reality and merged into infinity.

It is interesting to notice that important speakers—with great reputations whose influence reaches the public at large—mention this level of divine love. This universal love transcends the ego and the personality.

Dr. Wayne Dyer, renowned author and lecturer, dedicates an incredible amount of time to uplift, help and guide thousands of people through his talks on public television, his workshops and his books. Through his messages promoting creative thinking, he invites his public to open their minds and hearts to miracles, to create a new reality and to develop the superior degrees of love. He offers testimonies that are touching, particularly in his last book, *Wishes Fulfilled,* and through the weekend conferences, entitled *I Can Do It,* organized by his publisher, Hay House.

As well, one cannot ignore the many works by Dr. Deepak Chopra whose influence is well known. These highly qualified individuals become the bridge between an ordinary, limited life and a higher life we are called to live: the life of the soul and the spirit. No one can deny that a new consciousness is being born on the planet!

FRATERNAL CONSCIOUSNESS

Currently, we find ourselves at the frontier between two epochs: that which the Hindus call Kali Yuga and that of the New Era, or Age of Aquarius, which we are about to enter. According to the Mayan calendar, on December 21, 2012, the Earth will be in perfect alignment with the center of the Milky Way. This alignment marks the official beginning of the Aquarian Age and, at the same time, offers an exceptional opportunity to open our consciousness to the new currents. The consciousness of men has been, for a long period, in obscurity through the age of Kali Yuga, which was recognized by the Sages as the darkest age possible for spiritual development. For those ready to open their consciousness, they will receive the vibratory influences of the highest nature for their personal development and their spiritual blossoming.

The troubled and uncertain times that humanity is facing now invite us to seek, deeper within ourselves, the answers to fundamental questions. Who am I? What is the purpose of life? We are called to live so much more than a vegetative life such as a life of simply earning money, of yearning for more without decisive action to improve, grow and expand!

We live at the end of an epoch, the end of an old earth, an old consciousness that is selfish and materialistic. The waves of new cosmic energies present us with a ray of hope for our future. We have an invitation to transfer our energies from the inferior aspect, or the personality, to the divine aspect, or the individuality. It is an open door for all of us, beyond any race, color, or religion. It is an invitation for the realization of Self.

It will be a very long time before we have similar conditions or opportunities to make this quantum leap in our evolution. It is no wonder the planet is populated like never before in history; such rapid improvement of ourselves in one single lifetime present a unique opportunity.

From these new currents, the sixth race of human beings will be born with a more fraternal consciousness. With this new race, peace and harmony among nations will prevail.

> Even when we choose a higher level of consciousness, it may still be a product of the personality. We must reach the superconscious level, or the level of the *individuality*. The *individuality* is characterized by an expanded consciousness; we reach it only when we understand that all creatures, all life is one; that

all living creatures form a unity in the ocean of universal life in which all is immersed."[33]

Exercise: Pause and reflect for a moment and with sincerity and ardor, wish for universal love to dwell in your heart and cosmic light to shine in your mind.

Angel in the sky in New Zealand 2001 © Carmen Froment

---

33 Omraam Mikhaël Aïvanhov, *The Key to the problems of existence*, Complete Works, Vol. 11, France, Prosveta S.A., 1988, p. 25.

CHAPTER 7
Art: Source of Inspiration for the Soul

THE HISTORY OF MANKIND was depicted at first by art. This was followed by an epoch when religion dominated in the West, hindering the development of science and art. Eventually, religion declined and gave way to science, which is still in the forefront today. However, in the future, many expect that art will occupy first place again. Perhaps then we will understand the need for art once again to express itself in all of us.

Let us consider the three dimensions of form, content, and principles. Artists work to create the forms, i.e. the containers; mystics and religious people work at improving the ethical and psychic realm, i.e. the content; and the Initiates and great Masters work at the level of meaning, i.e. ideas and principles. Each plays a role in giving and nurturing the impetus to improve and perfect humanity.

In the way of thinking of the Initiates, art is an activity that can unify true science and true religion, each representing respectively the light and the warmth which bring divine creation.

Human beings are comprised of an *intellect* that corresponds to science and light, a *heart* that corresponds to religion and warmth, and a *will* that corresponds to art and creative activity, such as movement, composing, building, etc. In nature, these activities, dimensions, or components work together. In human nature, however, they are not always in balance. Often, the intellect, the heart, or the will work to the detriment of one another, resulting in suffering or even a serious imbalance.

Let us consider, for instance, people who manifest themselves through the intellect only. They will often be serious and cold engaging in endless dissertations and discussions to the point of arrogance. People who manifest themselves only from the emotional point of view are overly sensitive, get taken advantage of through lack of discernment, and possibly even get into trouble by giving way to passions and addictions. Their emotions become cloudy, dark, heavy, and sorrowful. People driven by willpower alone will often act without thinking or foreseeing the impact of their decisions on themselves or others. Their life path is often lopsided, like a vessel without any direction. When human beings are conscious of their inner trinity and are able to balance the activity of their intellect, heart, and will, the result is a more harmonious and balanced life.

Thanks to the Kirlian photography process, science now recognizes that the body is composed of a sensitive field of energy that reflects our thoughts and feelings. Beyond the skeletal, muscular, and nervous systems, the human body is composed of subtle bodies formed by thoughts, feelings, and aspirations. They are known as the *etheric* body, the *astral* body, and the *mental* body. In the esoteric tradition, it is said that what is below is like what is above. The lower trinity is a reflection of a higher trinity, our divine nature or Higher Self, but with a distortion, such as the image of a mountain reflected in a lake on a windy day.

This higher trinity is also endowed with subtle bodies, which are the *causal* body, the *buddhic* body, and the *atmic* body. They sustain the highest, most selfless thoughts, sublime feelings, and a sense of unity with all things. Through these bodies, we are in touch with our own divinity. Initiates from every generation have invited us to discover our true Self, to recapture our original image by working on our lower self in order to correct the distortion and merge our lower nature with our Higher Self, and to identify with our divine nature.

THE IMPORTANCE OF GESTURES

When human beings awaken to the awareness of their soul and spirit, and to the existence of a sublime world, everything starts changing in their vibrations and in their emanations. It is through these subtle bodies that we can connect with forces, currents, and entities throughout the universe—whether it is done consciously or unconsciously. It is said that magic is the science of gestures. So, it is important to pay attention to our gestures and movements while talking, moving, or even working so that we can remain in control of ourselves rather than being subject to unwanted influences.

Since gestures correspond to inner states, they are a means of observing oneself. Some gestures, reflexes for example, are so automatic they can barely be stopped at will. Sometimes gestures are performed unconsciously, under the influence of disharmonious currents. Self-observation is required to notice these patterns and to learn to control them. Gestures should be performed consciously allowing us to connect with beneficial currents and forces in the universe, to give blessings, or to receive inspirations.

Our hands and fingers are like antennas through which we can receive and transmit energies for painting, playing a musical instrument, sculpting, dancing, or healing. Hand gestures can make one feel confused and nervous or recharged, peaceful and magnetized. As the hands also represent willpower, it is possible to increase the mastery of our own gestures through simple exercises.

Master Omraam Aïvanhov suggests the following exercise: using the palm of your right hand, caress very gently the top of your left hand for a moment. Just feel the energy of your hands. With your right hand, use the thumb and next two fingers and caress delicately each finger of the left hand starting with the thumb and then the other fingers. Stay focused on the subtle energy emanating from your hands and fingers.

Our hands are the expression of our inner states, but conversely, they can also influence those inner states. We need to learn to work with them gently and consciously. Simple exercises, with this regard, are often very powerful. Paneurythmy[34] is a sacred dance where movements and music allow oneself to be renewed physically and emotionally. This wonderful expression of white magic allows us to learn how to use gestures, movements, and music to harmonize ourselves and express the new life—the life of the soul and the spirit.

Magic is defined as having an influence on another or on others as a result of a thought or an action. It is white magic when the influence is beneficial, such as bringing peace, light, or harmony. When the result is confusion, disorder, or dark feelings, it is considered black or diabolical magic.

In a way, we are all magicians because, through our way of living, we exercise an influence on our surroundings, on people, on nature, etc. It is therefore an important step in our awakening and progress to become aware of what we nourish ourselves with on all levels (physically, emotionally, mentally, and psychically) so that we can think, feel, and act in a more positive and harmonious way.

THE ACT OF CREATION

Master Aïvanhov explains that humans are driven to create and to surpass themselves:

> From the very beginning of his evolution, therefore, man has felt the need to create and, first and foremost, the need to create children. One of his strongest and most tenacious instincts is this need to be a creator and, in this way, to resemble his Heavenly Father. And if it is not children that he wants to create, it is works of art—sculptures, monuments, ballets, song, poems, etc. ... It [this desire] manifests itself as a need in man to transcend his own limits, to move onto a higher level and replace old forms by new,

---

34 The Paneurythmy was composed by the Bulgarian Master Peter Deunov at the beginning of the twentieth century and is now practiced in several countries.

subtler, more beautiful, more perfect forms. This is
a truth that many artists have failed to comprehend.
Man's creative powers belong to a higher plane than
his ordinary consciousness, to a region of his soul
that manifests itself as imagination, as the capacity
to explore and contemplate realities that transcend
him and to capture something of their elements. To
create is to transcend, to surpass oneself.[35]

Artists have a tremendous responsibility with regard to how
they influence others. They can become white magis if they dedicate
themselves and their talent to bringing humanity toward a higher
consciousness, to raising the vibration level to that of celestial realms,
and to awakening the divinity deep within people.

The soul is the daughter of God and the spirit is the son of God,
and in order to know them fully, in all their potential and splendor,
one has to reach up and aspire to live a divine life. This means a more
balanced life, a more harmonious life, with more purity in regard to
things that can nourish it, such as food, liquids, air, sounds, colors,
thoughts, feelings, and actions.

Art is a source of inspiration for the soul without a doubt, but
what do we mean by source? We can define source as the point at
which something springs into being, such as the beginning or place
of origin of a stream or river. So how do we trace the source of the
"Art Spring" in ourselves? We are all capable of being artistic. We all
have thoughts and feelings that are expressed through our actions
every minute. Think about when you feel love for your significant
other, parents, or children: sometimes you are so moved by their
presence or actions that you may write a poem or song to them or
about them. In these moments when the joy inside you rushes into
expression, you feel in touch with something precious. This grander
source is the God of your understanding that is constantly present
and is a constant gift.

---

35   Omraam Mikhaël Aïvanhov, *Cosmic Moral Laws*, Complete Works Vol.
     12, France, Prosveta, ed. 1989 pp. 55–56.

When was the last time you witnessed children coloring in a coloring book or painting with a brush that was bigger than their little hands? Edgar Degas said, "Painting is easy when you don't know how, but very difficult when you do." The intensity, focus, and oneness that children have with the colors they are applying is a true connection to a source inside that just wants, and ultimately loves, to express itself.

Don't you think everyone has this natural gift of being an artist? We have all had, at times, urges to run away from our problems, but as the great dancer and choreographer Twyla Tharp said, "Art is the only way to run away without leaving home."

So how do you enter the home of the artist inside you? How do you contemplate the divine riches that are there for you to draw out, dance out, sing out, or take your camera and capture the beauty of a sunrise?

Children sometimes tell their parents they want to become artists, and their parents tell them that it is not a good choice because they will make very little money, as if choosing to be an artist means being poor. When you live a vibrant life, connected to the Source (the God, the Master of your understanding) then no money can match up to the riches you feel inside. How can one put a price on an inner vision? How can one put a price on seeing something so beautiful in nature, that it makes you stop and contemplate your smallness in such immensity?

Imagine, for a brief moment, that on a specific night you go out with your spouse or friend to see an opera, attend a dance performance, or visit an art gallery. You wanted to go because your soul needed to be lifted to that platform inside you where rainbows, which have wrapped our dear Earth for so many years, come together in one moment of pure blessing. You can hear your inner voice whispering, "Yes! This is beautiful to watch, to listen to! The artist in me connects with the dignity of those artists. I consciously breathe in gratitude!"

And perhaps that night after the show, you find the language you speak with your beloved is elevated. Both of you are enthusiastically talking about what you just saw, what you felt from the expressive artists, and what you imagined was taking place. You have supported artists who have sculpted their inner sources to bring their gifts forward. You, in turn, treasure your own artist inside who appreciates such beauty. Perhaps that night you sleep better and have a wonderful dream. You wake up feeling vibrant and find yourself wanting to go on a nature hike and take photographs by a lake where you see your reflection and that of the trees and flowers. You seem more at peace with yourself and those with whom you live. You gave yourself the gift of allowing art to be a source of inspiration.

Master Aïvanhov gives us the following invitation: to strive each day to make our life purer, richer, and more luminous. In this way, we will subtly and imperceptibly lead all of creation heavenward.

When artistic creations act upon us in favorable ways, they inspire us and elevate our thoughts, feelings, and actions.

MUSIC

The experiments of a German physicist and musician, Ernst Chladni, in 1787, resulted in him discovering the lines of forces produced by sound. His technique consisted of drawing a bow over a piece of metal which surface was lightly covered with sand. The plate was bowed until it reached a precise tone and the sand formed a pattern showing the nodal regions. This discovery brought several other researchers to study the effect of sound on matter; today, this science is called *cymatics,* which is the study of visible sound and vibration, a subset of modal phenomena.

One could infer, therefore, that music can also affect us by creating harmonious or disharmonious lines of force that we cannot see, but feel. Experiments have demonstrated that a plant in an environment where heavy rock or metal music is played withers or dies in a relatively short time. Another experiment with milking cows showed that when Beethoven's music was played in the barn during the day, the cows produced a higher quality and quantity of milk.

Japanese author Masaru Emoto made the most interesting experiments regarding positive thinking and water droplets. He discovered that if human speech or thoughts are directed at water droplets before they are frozen, images of the resulting water crystals will be beautiful or ugly depending upon whether the words or thoughts were positive or negative. Mr. Emoto and colleagues have looked at environmental conditions, pollution, music type, and even thoughts and words, and have concluded thousands of experiments proving their research. We invite you to read his book entitled *The Hidden Messages of Water* (Bond Words Publishing, Inc., Hillsboro, Oregon, 2004).

Initiates from every generation have known and recognized the magical influence of sounds on human beings and on matter: it is reflected in such stories as the crumbling of the walls through the trumpets of Jericho and the myth of Orpheus with his lyre charming people and animals.

The music of an instrument or the voice of a singer can stimulate or weaken the willpower, enlighten or confuse the intellect, awaken higher feelings, or release vulgar passions. Musicians and singing artists have a great responsibility toward their audiences. Their art can elevate people or send them to their downfall.

When it comes to the art of music, we always have choices: to listen to music that irritates us or to turn it off. Why allow ourselves to be fed disharmony through music that is not elevating? Surely, at some point, we decided that it was time to search for music and sounds that were harmonious for our soul's thirst to be quenched.

Sacred music can be a powerful tool to support the imagination in bringing ideas into manifestation. When one knows how to listen to music, how to use its currents and movements, one can create an idea and project this idea onto the screen of the imagination to give forms, colors, and vivid pictures that, one day, will become realities. One becomes what one contemplates!

Inspired music, in particular, is the most accessible form of art. It is able to bring us closer to our heavenly home; it awakens a yearning for a lost paradise. When a singer, choir, or musician awakens the life of the soul and the spirit within us—or when we are brought to tears with an immense joy, like a fountain springing forth—we can say they have accomplished what the true mission of art is: awakening the divine world within.

Inspired, elevating music is the breath of the soul, of the consciousness. It is through music that the soul becomes alive and can help bring great harmony to earth.

All of us have witnessed the innate beauty and innocence of teenagers at some point in our lives. They seem to hold a presence that is tangible—yet intangible at the same time. They are living artists, deciding constantly what colors to wear through their clothing and in their hair—to feel beautiful, hip, or part of the larger picture they live in. They giggle, gossip, and seem to have a fraternal love for each other. They often move with grace and acceptance of the art that lives in them. They are untouchable at some point. They are a living painting coming into form. You might say this is thinking of teenagers in an idealistic way because they are not like that anymore! Possibly, but, if we see them through the eyes of an artist, we can see such beauty in everyone—everywhere and at any age. Surely, as teenagers, we also felt that we could be as one with everything. Most of us have had times when we felt larger than life. We felt indispensable or connected to everything around us.

How do artists become inspired? What is inspiration? Inspiration is a subtle element that comes from a higher region, uplifts the artists, and allows them, through their musical instrument or their medium, to produce something brilliant. Artists do not necessarily know where it comes from or how it proceeds. They try to learn to think, feel, and act in a clear way to attract the elements of inspiration, so that heavenly currents will nourish their soul and spirit and allow them to elevate others to those regions where they feel transported, uplifted, and united with the sacred.

Remember the first time you saw time-lapse photography and you witnessed the opening of a rose in slow motion? Wasn't that magnificent? The beauty of a flower opening is happening every day, every nanosecond. The living force that is unseen and manifests itself into such great art forms in nature is a constant source of inspiration.

Mother Nature is undoubtedly a great source of inspiration for us all. E. E. Cummings expressed his profound joy in appreciating this when he wrote, "I thank you God for this most amazing day:

for the leaping greenly spirits of trees and for the blue true dream of sky; and for everything which is natural which is infinite which is yes."[36]

We always come back to nature. Even during interactions with others, if there is a lull in the conversation, people will say something about the weather. If they comment that the weather is wonderful, then perhaps this joyful news sparks more joyful exchanges in conversation. Or, the opposite can be true: after people talk about how bad the weather is, they will often speak about how unhealthy they are. So, inevitably we come back to nature. We rely on our instincts to stay connected to nature—that awe-inspiring force that lives and breathes its abundance of light into us. If we are open and receptive, we retrieve the gifts from nature; if we are closed and cut off, we miss them. Yet nature is still there waiting and ready to pour its beauty into our eyes, hearts, and hands.

In fact, we can find art everywhere in nature: from the delicate beauty of flowers, the singing of birds, the chant of a waterfall, the whispering of the wind, the natural carving of rocks, or the glow of snowy summits. True poetry is everywhere in nature; the Word takes expression through forms, sounds, and colors.

Khalil Gibran said, "And forget not that the earth delights to feel your bare feet and the winds long to play with your hair."[37]

Our minds create thoughts and ideas, representing the masculine principle that is linked to the sun, but the imagination gives form, acting as the feminine principle, the formative power linked to the moon. It is important to remember that the role of this wonderful faculty called imagination is to give form and shape, like a woman giving form to the child in her womb. Cosmic intelligence has made these faculties available for us to learn, develop, and use to their full potential. Artistic creation should not be the result of an imagination gone wild. Psychiatric wards and asylums are already too busy with people who have let their imaginations go astray. Imagination, a feminine principle, is available to us all, man and woman, so that we

---

36 *E. E. Cummings: Complete Poems, 1904–1962,* New York, Liveright, 1994, p. 663.

37 Khalil Gibran, *The Prophet,* New York, Alfred A. Knopf, 2009, p. 36.

can nurture, develop, and bring to fruition the ideas generated by our intellect—a masculine principle.

Another element that many of us may have felt at one point or another, without necessarily recognizing it, is the influence of the moon. Artists who are particularly sensitive may feel this influence on their emotions and their imagination: during the waxing moon, they may feel more positive and enthusiastic, whereas during the waning moon, they may feel more negativity or even apathy. And, of course, the images in their imagination during these times could influence their work. However, if they are aware of these influences in nature, instead of being subject to negative moods, they can rise above them through psychic work by linking with the energies of the sun, which as always is filled with light, warmth, and life!

In general, the criterion for beauty is different for each individual because we live in a varied society. Attention is mostly focused on outside activities without being too aware of what is going on inside. If we are aware of our inner structure and are in touch with the world of unity, we can recognize that unity in all things; we can know the ultimate criteria of beauty as the Sages and great Masters do. They see beauty as the expression of the cosmic principle that the Divine Mother represents.

Artists suggest that, through their art, they wish to represent their inner reality. However, that reality sometimes conveys only distress and pessimism. It reveals a sadness that can affect the hearing, cause confusion, and leave a feeling of depression. Of course, they create their own reality, but why expose it for everyone to see? Some will say that it is best to be realistic. Of course, but why feed on garbage when a delicious dish is available? Why not simply explore colors, forms, and sounds that awaken a soothing or stimulating sensation and are vivifying! Why go back to the primordial chaos? Why not choose the opposite process that takes place in nature: that from which chaos, life, order, beauty, and perfection are born, like a water lily emerging from muddy waters? Too many artists depict their art by reflecting the infernal layers of the subconscious regions.

We are all responsible for the influence we have on others. The way we think, feel, and act produces emanations, radiations, and vibrations that we carry with us and around us. The work of the artist is a reflection of his or her thoughts and emotions. A ray of sunshine making its way through a pure crystal will emerge as pure, luminescent, and showing magnificent colors, but if the crystal is opaque and faulty, the colors will be dull or absent.

If the ideal of artists is only to make money, become famous, or feed their vanity, their influence is at risk of becoming mediocre and can be devastating. From an initiatic perspective, they also put themselves at risk of losing their talent because they cut themselves from the source, the world of sublime inspiration.

If artists would take a moment before beginning their work and pray that their talent be used to improve themselves and to enlighten, warm, and vivify others, they would be supported by the invisible world. Higher beings would come and inspire them. Nothing is more sublime than wanting to bring people closer to heaven. If artists nourished the ideal of elevating their souls and bringing people back to the source, closer to perfection, their names would be inscribed in the Book of Life.

The soul and the spirit are equipped with antennae prepared to communicate with heaven. To create a masterpiece according to the highest criteria, artists need to surpass themselves, touch the celestial regions, and capture their subtle elements in order to reproduce these elements and distribute them through their art. The greatest secret for the artist is to know that art is a call to surpass oneself, to bring something better to mankind. Art is the best tool and the best way to nurture our progression toward the divinity and to awaken that divinity in others. That is what is meant by "divine creations" and "divinely inspired art works."

In the future, art will recapture first place. This is one of the only forms of expression capable of awakening the desire to live a better life where divine wisdom and divine love exist. Aïvanhov once said: "In the future, artists will rank first in human society, for a true artist is a priest, philosopher and scientist."[38]

---

38 Omraam Mikhaël Aïvanhov, *Creation: Artistic and Spiritual*, Izvor Collection, # 223, France, Prosveta S.A., ed. 1988 p. 7.

The true mission of art is to bring human beings back to the lost paradise and to awaken the superconsciousness in them. The best way to improve mankind is in the hands of artists. Their role is to represent on the physical plane what their intelligence conceives as truth and what their hearts feel to be good in order to allow the divine to find expression into matter.

Whether it is through poetry, music, or singing, art should awaken in us the memory of the celestial regions: where we come from and where we shall return one day. When art sets in motion the vibrations of the most highly spiritual chords of our being, we receive an impetus to create a new life and reach toward perfection.

> Any creation born of a disinterested idea and used for the purpose of an impersonal cause possesses the germ of immortality. He who is aware of this law is in a position to acquire true wealth, for the one achievement that is above all others is to win a soul for the light.[39]

ART BEGINS WITH US

Idealization is a means of mastering one's inner state by drawing a world of beauty from the imagination. It is an extraordinary way to open new paths for self-transformation. In Hinduism, Jnana Yoga is the practice of idealization through which adepts access a superior reality and identify with their divine nature, their Higher Self.

Many believe that it is an illusion to try to identify with one's Christ-like nature. Initiates, on the contrary, believe that it is an illusion to identify oneself with one's weaknesses, vices, and illnesses. They do not deny the reality we live in; they maintain that this reality is a temporary imprisonment from which we must learn to free ourselves in order to enjoy a true reality which is stable, immortal, and celestial. Why not choose the most liberating illusion? If we nourish a sublime ideal, if we make it the center of our existence with all our heart and soul, this ideal will protect us, enlighten us, and

---

39   Ibid, p. 77.

give us a sense of direction. It will act as a living force, nurturing us with elements of its own nature. Initiates have known it forever: *we become what we contemplate!*

Art is an open path to heaven; true art, as understood by the Sages and Initiates, is to work on oneself. To become artistic every day is to learn to sculpt oneself, to express oneself like a poem, and to move as in a dance. At present, we stand like unfinished paintings, but when we create an image of ourselves pictured as in the depths of our being, we become the most valuable artists in the eyes of Heaven. In this way, we work for our own good, drawing on the riches of our divine Self to help those riches become a solid reality within us, on the physical plane. We can say that we participate in the realization of a new Earth—the Earth of the living! And the masterpieces we create will never disappear; we shall carry them with us for eternity.

The art of the future will be an expression of our own sculpting, our own painting, to be warm, expressive, and alive. We will awaken in people what they seek most in themselves: light, love, and divine life.

The greatest canvas we can find is our very own nature. We have all been given free will. Let us use it wisely. Why not create a bank of consciousness wherein we can deposit ideal thoughts, dreams, or celestial desires such as being touched by an Angel? The deposits will become pure gold running in our veins; it will be available to us through meditation, contemplation, and prayer. By offering the colors of our inner palette to the spirit, we can express our imagination through our gestures and words.

Through our smiles, thoughts, and actions, we become everyday artists. We sculpt ourselves through positive and luminous choices. We dance and sing our joy and gratitude. Art is a source of inspiration! We are all artists, and we can all become a source of inspiration to each other!

> The artist *par excellence* is he who takes his own flesh
> as material for his sculpture, his own face and body
> as a canvas on which to paint, his own thoughts
> and feelings as clay to be modeled. He wants all

the beauty and harmony of creation to flow and be expressed through his being. An artist such as this creates the art of the new culture which is dawning in the world.[40]

Exercise: Affirmation: With all your attention, your intent and your strength repeat the following affirmation, knowing that thousands of other people are saying it daily:

To have a heart as pure as crystal,
A mind as luminous as the sun
A soul as vast as the universe
A spirit as powerful as God and
One with God.

Dove and Crystal © Prosveta S.A.

---

40   Ibid p. 173

CHAPTER 8
Nature and Its Changes

WE ARE THE HOLOGRAPHIC image of the cosmos. The universe represents the macrocosm, and human beings represent the microcosm. The great and the small are intimately related through the same principles and are subject to the same laws that can be observed throughout nature.

To ensure our survival, we must make some exchanges with the cosmos and with nature. These exchanges can be through the air we breathe, the water we drink, the food we eat, and the respect and considerations we give to the earth. Without these exchanges with nature, we face death. Nature is therefore our nurturing mother—not only on the physical plane but also on the psychic and spiritual levels. Thanks to nature, we learn how to grow, blossom, and become as one with her. If we open our hearts, we feel connected with her. Being a part of her, we will feel her generosity, greatness, splendor, and complicity with the Creator.

Furthermore, she will open herself up to us, revealing the laws that sustain her and the principles that animate them. Nature is the source of the great cosmic truths to which we are equally bound.

THE WORLD OF PRINCIPLES

It is said in *initiatic science* that the principles are very few, but they govern the numerous world of laws—and these govern the world of manifestations, which are infinite. From unity is born diversity.

From the principles governing the universe, nature, and human beings, we can say that everything begins with the One, that is the central point, the Creator, the primordial dimension, the Spirit. From there, the point stretches to become a line and becomes polarized with its two extremities: the two principles are born—the masculine and the feminine, light and warmth (father, mother)—from where the energies begin to circulate; it is the wheel set in motion from which movement is born (the child). We now have a trinity, the three principles, which are also found in the human being as the intellect, the heart, and willpower. In our evolution they are represented by the development of the equilateral triangle of wisdom, love and truth.

So far, in the world of principles, we have unity, duality, and trinity. From these principles, all the laws and their applications follow.

THE WORLD OF LAWS

When we observe how nature maintains its balance through the law of polarity, through opposites, of duality such as the negative and the positive, spirit, and matter, above and below, day and night, we notice that, through these opposites, each plays a necessary role to complement the manifestation of the other.

The law of causes and consequences is the foundation of morality. It is also known as the law of action and reaction (what you sow, you shall reap). In nature, no one can deny that agriculture is the best example of this law. No one expects to reap figs on a vine! This law governs the applications of karma, reincarnation, and destiny.

Another important law is the law of recording. Everything is recorded in nature as it is composed of a very subtle substance by which all vibrations, emanations, and radiations are recorded.

Therefore, from this law of recording comes the law of affinity as all the particles of the same nature are attracted together. "Birds of a feather flock together."

Then comes the law of echo, or the boomerang effect: if you stand on a mountain and say, "I love you," you hear the echo say, "I love you, I love you." We can say that these three laws are the three magic laws. If we learn to observe them in nature—to apply them in our reasoning, our thinking, and our behavior—we shall live a new life in harmony with nature and the entire cosmos.

There are many more laws: the law of giving and taking, the law of sacrifice, the law of attraction, the law of necessity, and other universal laws which we shall cover later in this chapter. Let us go now to the world of manifestations.

WORLD OF MANIFESTATIONS

The manifestations or applications of the principles and the laws are written everywhere in nature. If the universe and nature are governed by the same principles and the same laws—and if we are a part of the universe and nature—it means by extrapolation, deduction, and holography, that we are subject to the same principles and laws in all three worlds: the physical plane, the psychic plane, and the spiritual plane. In *The Emerald Table*, Hermes Trismegistus said, "Everything that is below is like that which is above, and everything that is above is like that which is below."

Let us see how the world of principles applies in matter and in our lives. The principle of unity reveals that all of creation was born from a thought of the Creator—the invisible, infinite, unlimited principle. This is rather difficult for us to comprehend! The Infinite cannot be contained in the finite and to get to know it, we must travel through the other principles, laws, and applications in order to come back to the primordial unity.

Let's carry on with the principle of duality by taking the most obvious example: day and night. We all love the sun as it gives us light and warmth. It allows us to see, admire colors in nature, and to move about with ease as the light is there to guide us. But, thanks to the night and its obscurity, the greatness, immensity, and infinity of creation too can be revealed.

Nature continually speaks to us, showing us the way of our own development. Numerous analogies are described in the *Dictionary of the Book of Nature*,[41] based on the conferences given by Omraam Mikhaël Aïvanhov for nearly half a century.

Take only the example of a seed. When it is put in the soil, it stays down—literally in the dark and the cold (for a while)—and then its shell cracks open to rot so to speak, until the germ sprouts and pushes through the soil, reaching up toward the light. The same thing happens with the mother carrying the child in the darkness of her womb; without this preparation phase in the dark, life cannot spring forth.

> You might say that light is the daughter of darkness. The child, after all, emerges from the womb of its mother, not the other way around. Light is incapable of giving birth to obscurity, on the contrary light dissipates obscurity. But obscurity gives birth to light. How this can be is a mystery: the mystery of movement. Without movement, there is no light.[42]

We can now transpose this relationship to our own existence when we are forced by life's circumstances to reflect and reevaluate our priorities. On the physical, emotional or psychic plane, when we go through a hard time or a great suffering, we can say that we are going through a stage of darkness yet when we observe more closely we find that it is often followed by a feeling of deep peace. If the stage of darkness and cold is difficult to face, it is still a very important step to bring about a new awareness. From darkness, the light is born; from suffering, the light is also born—a revealing light under the form of knowledge, new wisdom or possibly a revelation.

---

41 Published in French through Prosveta France in the Spring of 2012.
42 Omraam Mikhaël Aïvanhov, *The Living book of Nature*, Izvor collection #216, France, Prosveta, ed. 1984, p. 29.

The great Sages and Saints knew of this experience as the dark night of the soul: the soul is calling for something more and the ego does not want to give up its place. At first, an inner fight or resistance takes place, but if a being emerges triumphant, an opening takes place in his/her consciousness. A gift of great awareness, clarity, or grace follows.

Take the example of the diamond and how it grows in the depths of the earth. It begins as a molecule of pure carbon. Under great pressure—for a long time, in the darkness—it forms itself into one of the most precious stones on earth. Through our various trials in life, we are put under greater or lesser pressure. At present, it is on the collective level that we undergo a greater pressure. Doesn't life offer us sometimes the perfect conditions to become precious stones?

Day and night, all of nature is sustained by a powerful life composed of pure light and, if our eyes are capable of supporting the light of the day, they could not support the living light without a preparation phase. We would be certainly blinded. This light, that we could say is spiritual, is of such a refined nature, so powerful, that our ordinary senses are not prepared to capture it. We have no idea of the strength or the tension that would be felt if we could see the true nature of all creation with its primordial light. It is by studying nature, by observing it, contemplating it, by appreciating it, that it will reveal itself in all its beauty. It shall be Isis unveiled!

The second most striking example linked to the law of polarity is the activity between the two principles, masculine and feminine. In the universe, everything is connected in perfect harmony, and the two principles work hand in hand to allow life to circulate. With human beings, the most evident manifestation of these two principles is directly linked to men and women—although each exists within the potential of the other. It is the memory of their original unity that brings them to seek each other on the outside. However, it is primarily from within that one must seek to develop the complementary principle in order to find a harmonious relationship and even become androgynous, like the great Masters and Initiates who can accomplish marvels thanks to the balanced development of these two principles.

Let us consider what happens when there is a polarity imbalance in atmospheric conditions: when the electric charge in the air is too much, a storm or rain causes change to the conditions and magnetizes the atmosphere. It is the same with us when there is an imbalance in our own polarity.

Nature speaks to us all the time, and it tries to warn us if we know how to listen and read her messages. Mother Nature records everything; when we abuse nature, eventually she sends a great flood, earthquake, or volcanic eruption to regain her balance. Isn't it the same with us when we abuse food and drink or become too tired or stressed? We become indisposed until we right the imbalances in ourselves.

Each important event we have to live through is generally preceded by warning signs. But as we do not know the language of nature, we do not know how to read the messages brought to us by the four elements, or by plants, animals, humans or particular dreams. Every event is preceded by certain signs, just like those detected with the aid of scientific instruments before earthquakes, volcanic eruptions, cyclones and tidal waves.

The universe is one, so there are connections, communications, between all its constituent elements, just as in our physical body the state of one organ affects all the others. And so any event occurring in any part of the world emits vibrations, which spread throughout space and are perceived by certain beings. These beings are able to pick up the vibrations and are, therefore, the first to be warned. And we also receive warnings with regard to our inner life.[43]

---

43 Omraam Mikhaël Aïvanhov, *Daily Meditations*, France, Prosveta, ed. 2011, for March 18, 2012, p. 84.

THE ABUSES OF NATURE

As we know, the earth, sea, water, and air are involved in the production of food. However, pollution is threatening our resources—all fundamental and indispensable to life. The effect of the sun is altered through the thinning of the ozone layer. Animal and vegetable species are quickly disappearing, and the climatic changes are reducing agricultural production for an increasing population now surpassing seven billion inhabitants! Let's not forget the acceleration of the melting of the polar caps, which affects an already precarious balance. Will the disappearance of these polar caps risks shifting the axis of the planet?

Moreover, the overconsumption of fast food, packaged drinks, and products of all kinds contribute to garbage pollution. If everyone took time to reevaluate their priorities, simplify their needs, and slow down, it would at least begin the deceleration of the destructive process of our precious Mother Earth.

To the environmental crisis, add the human crisis—as much as on the consciousness, thinking, or physical level. Our own consciousness is clouded by mental pollution. We are blinded by the fast pace of the modern world. How can we remove the mental pollution and find some clarity through all of our busy-ness? Maybe, by studying the laws of living nature and evaluating our priorities on a longer term, we will think more clearly and our actions will be more constructive and beneficial not only to ourselves but also to those whom we work or associate with on a daily basis.

Despite all this, we can act positively. In nature, all poison offers an antidote. Even with a homeopathic dose, a poison can become a cure. The same thing applies on a psychic level. Any situation that appears chaotic or disastrous holds a solution—possibly of renewal. If we all link together in consciousness and decide to take a step forward by accepting a willingness to change some of our behavior to assure the protection of nature, we shall contribute on a human level, as with homeopathic remedies, to establish new sets of criteria for a better environmental ethic.

By simplifying our mental activities, our way of eating, living and working, our consciousness is lighter, freer, and more open. A new awareness respecting the laws that govern nature—and us as well—cultivates a new, sustainable attitude. By maintaining this new awareness, we see a new heaven and a new earth which are a new consciousness and a new behavior!

When we are deaf to the calling of nature, it manifests itself through its allies. The four elements (fire, air, water, and earth) work together to maintain a balance far beyond our very own existence. A mother who educates her child and repeats her rules might have to reprimand or maybe even whip (symbolically speaking, of course) her child. The four elements over the millenniums set things in motion and release some form of cataclysm, which is usually only a means of correction to ensure a renewal.

Aren't these climatic changes a way for nature to warn us of the consequences of our mistakes and abuses and to teach us a way to find a better balance for the future of our planet and our own existence? It brings us back to proper order. All the changes taking place in nature force us to constantly adapt and modify our behavior. When things become unstable, human beings are obliged to find new reference points, and the intellect is obliged to recognize its incapacity to explain or foresee everything. Maybe then it is willing to listen to the intuition and work in harmony with the heart. Already, you've noticed the incredible help that stems from people following a natural disaster; people open their hearts, move beyond analytical reasoning, forget about themselves, and immediately go to alleviate the suffering.

Have you noticed, in the past decade or so, how time seems to accelerate and the pressures to mount? In the present chaos and disorder, we may be invited to prepare our physical body and our consciousness for a new focus, as if a better life was calling on us. This tension develops our nervous system to sustain the power of light. We do not know it ourselves yet, but the Sages and Initiates who have developed their subtle bodies and have traveled through space tell us that the true nature, the one of all creation is composed of that primordial, spiritual light. Everything is light!

We must wake up, understand, and move forward. When we make up our minds, set a practice and take conscious action, this will produce an impetus, a love, from which is born an understanding, light, and wisdom.

SOLUTIONS

When reading the living book of nature, we find a thousand solutions to the problems that are presently weighing down humanity. Here is a marvelous example that Mother Nature offers us, so evident, but which no one thinks about; it could be the solution to all our problems. It concerns the migration of birds in general—and wild geese in particular. Each bird creates an updraft for the one following it. By flying in a V formation, the autonomy of the group is increased by 71 percent; every bird receives the energy of the collective formation, and the entire flock receives the benefit of the collective effort. The geese know that when they leave the formation, they will have to fight the aerodynamic resistance of the air, so they recognize the necessity of remaining united for the ultimate goal of reaching their destination.

Could we make an analogy with the high ideal? The geese replace each other at the head of the formation, which shows an incredible sense of responsibility in the sharing of the tasks and demanding obligations. And when they assume the rear position, they encourage those flying ahead with their calls. If one of them is hurt, two others will come to help and protect it—and they will even wait until it gets better or dies before they go back to the formation. Does it not make sense to help and support each other in difficulty? Don't they give us a perfect solution for the future of humanity?

Many people already apply these solutions by choosing to create a new awareness, by changing their habits and behavior. Just take the example of the recent exponential growth of organic agriculture, vegetarianism, and recycling throughout the four corners of the planet. It is an extraordinary awakening in such short a time!

Here is another way of helping humanity and the planet: adopting a healthy way of living and eating that will alleviate many illnesses and eradicate polluting industries. Also, by becoming vegetarians, we learn to respect life, protect the life of the animals, and fortify our bodies. We begin to eat with a sense of appreciation so the elements we absorb contribute to our health on all levels.

And then one should consider the management of one's own time. Working as we do now is motivated by gain and consumerism; should it not basically just meet the necessities of life? If we took time every day to appreciate nature through walks by blooming gardens, springs, or waterfalls, not only would our bodies be more oxygenated, but our thinking would also be clearer. Moreover, the contemplation of beauty and meditation on the greatness of creation would nourish our souls and spirits, which are often forgotten or neglected. In fact, everybody is seeking happiness but always through external means or possessions without taking into consideration the inner structure where the soul and spirit need to be nourished. The soul and spirit are the ones holding the keys to lasting happiness.

If everyone decided to work inwardly, using the power of the creative mind, to nourish a sense of self-development, harmony and brotherhood, a peace would emerge from the soul and the spirit. True peace begins first within oneself. Instead of focusing on the religious or spiritual differences, we should adopt a universal spirituality: a unique solar approach, since the sun is the giver of life, light, and warmth. It is impersonal, grandiose, and stable—and it teaches us to overcome our prejudices and become the model it is. Little by little, the wars of religion and the churches of different cults would disappear for a lasting peace. The love for each other and the fraternity between nations would bring harmony and eliminate all armed conflicts and jails.

Why not take a few minutes as soon as we wake up to harmonize ourselves with the divine program for the day? It is only a matter of letting go of our worries and elevating our being to the level of our Higher Self, which is always ready to protect us and guide us through intuition. Moreover, if before we begin our daily obligations, we took a brief moment to honor nature by saluting it and thanking it for the life it brings us, it would reveal itself through our gratitude.

Nature shows us how to develop the heart through its beauty and greatness. It holds the greatest truths, which are revealed in the form of a synthesis that intuition recognizes. When the intellect is too dominant, it often becomes destructive because, through its analysis, it shreds things and divides them. Whereas, with the warmth of the heart working together with the light of the intellect in a balanced manner, the truth is born! The sun shows us that through its warmth and light, which give birth to life!

If we learn to balance these three activities of the heart, the intellect, and the will on all levels—physical, moral, and spiritual— our blossoming is guaranteed just as nature assures the blossoming of all species through the warmth, light, and life of the sun.

Maybe we are separated from one another through oceans and mountains—or born of different cultures—but if we develop a collective awareness, we shall obtain the true power. The awareness of unity becomes the foundation for true morale.

Let us become like a spring that flows and vivifies everything in its path. The spring within us is love. When we connect with the source, we feel purified, nourished, and vivified. It awakens in us our own spring so it can water our inner garden and help the sprouting of the divine seeds deposited in the depth of our souls.

This spring is love—it is life—and it is the magnetism of the universe. Without love, the universe would disintegrate. Love is the greatest universal law, and it only seeks to flow, to water, and to vivify everything on its way.

Exercise: Visualize a spring that flows from the sun; it cascades down and floods you with its purity, its light, its warmth. Let this spring flow through your cells and your organs. Feel yourself renewed, refreshed, invigorated, and becoming a living spring!

Cascade © Claude Brun

CHAPTER 9
Aquarius: Fusion of the Religions

*"In the beginning was the Word, and the Word was
with God, and the Word was God. The same was in the
beginning with God. All things were made by him; and
without him was not anything made that was made."*
—John 1:1–2

ASTROLOGY IS THE STUDY of the relationship between planetary cycles and human affairs on earth. It seeks to establish correspondences between large cosmic cycles and the evolutionary journey humanity is passing through during each given epoch.

Each cycle has specific influences on human destiny and helps shape the social, political, economic, intellectual, and spiritual structures of an era or epoch. Therefore, we can say that the science of astrology is based on the life rhythm and pulsations of a solar system.

In the study of ancient sacred texts, astrologers believed that, in order to obtain a solar system with the best possible organization, the superior entities who took charge of it had to establish limitations and rules that no one could transgress without consequences. Any action, feeling and thought is recorded and registered in what is known as Akasha Chronica.

> Initiatic Science teaches that we live out our lives immersed in the ocean of fluidic matter known as astral light. This fluid is so sensitive that it bears the record of everything that occurs in the universe: the most insignificant gesture, the slightest, most superficial emotion, every fleeting thought that goes through our minds: it is all recorded. [...] It is this fluidic matter that Hermes Trismegistus referred to as Telesma. [...] The Hindu name for this fluidic matter is Akasha. [...] This fluid, therefore, this Akasha on which everything is recorded, in which everything is reflected, reaches to the limits of the universe, and these limits are represented for us by the belt of the zodiac.[44]

In observing the stars, we can discover what happened in the distant past, draw conclusions, and even predict the future. The ancient astrologers acknowledged the science of astronomy and created a symbolic language to express that past and future. They called it the zodiac. Symbols are the living language of the Initiates.

When someone observes a planet or a sign, the definition and understanding differs, according to the state of being of that observer; this is one of the reasons why there are so many interpretations in astrology. When the key to the degrees is taken into consideration by astrologers, this science is precise because it based on the knowledge, the initiatic knowledge modeled on immutable principles and archetypes.

At the head of the zodiac stands the one named by esoteric science as the First Son. He is the Thinker, the creative Word, and, in the sacred language, we know him under the name of the Cosmic Christ. He is symbolized by a triangle with an eye that sees everything. The ancient civilizations, particularly those from South America and Egypt, gave him the name Sun God. In the Christian

---

44 Omraam Mikhaël Aïvanhov, *The Zodiac, Key to Man and to the Universe*, Izvor Collection # 220, France, Prosveta SA, ed. 1986, pp. 11–13.

religion, he is represented in the communion by the host and wine. According to the esoteric science this great Cosmic Being sacrificed himself to give life to our solar system. To better focus the energies of the zodiac, this Cosmic Christ, established his realm at the center, i.e. the heart of the solar system, the Sun.

The Sun symbolizes the heart, vitality, and the energy of the Father in astrology; he is the ruler of the Leo sign, the king of animals. Leo is in opposition to Aquarius, symbolized by a water-bearer, pouring water over the earth.

The axis Aquarius-Leo is in relation to the cold and the warmth respectively. Leo represents the creative fire, the house of the Sun, warmth, and love. Aquarius, for his part, is governed by Saturn, the cold of wisdom, and also by Uranus represented by truth, linked to the eyes. In antiquity, Uranus was represented by an eye flying above the ocean. Therefore, the Aquarian age dawning will be a period during which love and wisdom will be in the first place; they will be at the foundation of a new life and a new culture. Humanity will be able to find truth because truth is born from love and wisdom.

> This is why the Aquarius-Leo axis (which will be the active influence in the world henceforth, since we are just entering the Age of Aquarius) represents the new era in which disciples and all children of God will work with the love of the Sun (Leo) and the wisdom of Saturn (Aquarius) and live in the truth brought by Uranus. […] Christ is the Sun, Christ is the heart pouring out its blood, its love, into the whole universe.[45]

THE GREAT YEAR CYCLE: LEAVING THE PISCEAN AGE

The "Great Year" is a term used to describe the cycle of the backward shifting point of equinox against the backdrop of the twelve constellations. The gradual precession of the equinox has to do with the earth's rotation about the ecliptic pole, the gravitational

---

45   Ibid, pp. 107–109.

attraction of the sun and moon, and the fact that the earth is not a perfect circle; it bulges somewhat around the equator.

One complete revolution of the vernal equinox takes roughly 25,920 years, and this period is called the Great Year. When we divide the Great Year by the twelve constellations (zodiac signs), we obtain 2,160 years for the vernal equinox point to move through a sign. These periods are known as the processional or astrological ages.

At the present time, we are in the last degrees of the Piscean Era. More than two thousand years ago, an historical being known as Jesus of Nazareth was born. This being was different than most; he had to have gone through special initiations in previous lives and, thanks to his efforts and great purity, he gave his body to this great solar entity, the Christ, for three years. He was not alone to accomplish such work; with the support of the Great White Brotherhood of the Elders from the Himalaya, the Master Jesus made a huge sacrifice.

We must differentiate between Jesus of Nazareth and the Christ to have a better idea of what he represents for Earth. The spirit of Christ ran through the pouring of Jesus' blood to enable him to free humanity from a negative collective karma. Despite this liberation, believing in Jesus does not mean that we are automatically saved because human beings need to also learn sacrifice!

The era of Pisces brought great progress in all realms of life, but it is only a beginning. Christ stayed in a physical body on Earth for three years, but he did not abandon humanity. The earth we walk upon, the food we eat, the air we breathe, and the warmth of the sun we feel are wholly impregnated with the Christ energy.

The efforts we make for ourselves are important stepping stones for the development of our consciousness. The sign of Pisces is ruled by Neptune and Jupiter. In Greek mythology, they are known as Poseidon, the God of the Sea, and Zeus, the God of Heaven. That implies that the Piscean Area was largely ruled by water, linked to the emotions and feelings, and by Heaven, which governs Spirit, the divine world.

In the fixed zodiac, the sign of Pisces is opposite to the sign of Virgo. Pisces is the sign corresponding to feelings and divine love; Virgo corresponds to health and work, which is also symbolized by the solar plexus. One can observe that, during the Piscean era, human beings developed considerably on the level of ideas, thoughts, and exterior innovations, but they have not yet learned to develop their subtle senses and their inner earth.

In the religious language, many think they must save their souls to go to heaven and live in paradise or in nirvana. But, where is the earth in all that? In the realms of science, art, and religion, we can observe the result of this philosophy as we have forgotten the reason of our existence on earth. We exploit it; we take from it without giving anything in return, unaware of the existence of invisible beings behind what we see physically.

DAWNING OF AQUARIUS

It is impossible to determine the exact crossover point from one sign to the next, but it is generally thought of as a gradual shift from one age to the next with a sort of overlap of about 100–200 years. Today, we find ourselves at the threshold between the setting Age of Pisces and the rising Age of Aquarius. This means that the prevailing values that have shaped the Age of Pisces will give way to principles and ideals represented by Aquarius.

One of the new influences related to the Aquarian era is that human beings will become aware of their guides and the spirits of the invisible world with whom they will learn to fully collaborate. Divine life and its applications will be understood from within and quite differently than in the past.

The influence of Aquarius will be felt in all areas of life. For each epoch, in order for a sign to take on full manifestation, a highly evolved being must incarnate on earth by taking possession of a physical body. This being integrates the corresponding energy to the sign and brings it to its full potential, so that all of humanity can benefit from it.

In Aquarius, the realm of feelings, which is linked to the heart, will unite with the realm of thoughts linked to the intellect.

They will work hand in hand on the path of intuition. Saturn and Uranus are the two masters of the Aquarius sign. Saturn, through its influence, will bring structure and organization; it will bring people to become responsible with matter without infringing the laws of nature. And Uranus will open the doors to the invisible world so that people's minds open up to higher ideals; it will allow them to adopt a behavior that disassociates them from the animal kingdom, particularly in regard to the law of the fittest.

Everything that has been accomplished in the Piscean era will not be forgotten or vanish. The era of Aquarius will be a period of going deeper within. It will allow the Cosmic Water coming from the Universal Soul to come down on earth as represented in the symbol of Aquarius.

Aquarius is a human sign in close relationship to the needs of humanity. Related to Saturn, it will bring order, peace, and harmony for the good of the collectivity. In addition, religion, art, and science will no longer operate separately; they will complement each other.

There is another important detail to make about the axis Leo-Aquarius in the zodiac: the sign of Leo, related to the Sun and to creativity, will tend toward a collective expression in the future rather than to personal growth that fed the egoist interests in the past. Aquarius will help develop the common good without losing one's personal identity in the collectivity. There will be a net improvement of life's conditions on earth—even though there will still be some rich and poor people. We will become aware of the fact that true riches are within and that we can access those riches by abolishing the limitations we built. We shall no longer discriminate against people based on their color, race, or country but will consider them as a single race, a single family, humanity. This new understanding will help us see that the erroneous philosophy keeping us separated—isolated, believing that we only had one existence—will no longer be sustainable in the Aquarian Age.

> Above, in the Heavenly regions, they [people] are
> all built on the same pattern with the same organs,
> the same capacities and needs, the same desires and

the same ideal. [...] As human beings evolve they will gradually know each other better and see that, inwardly, they are all alike: they all aspire to joy, happiness and freedom, to knowledge and light, and they all experience suffering in the same way. [...] If the countries that are at war with each other in the world today suddenly became aware that they all belonged to the one, Heavenly homeland, they would stop massacring each other.[46]

With the dawning of the Aquarian Age, human beings will realize they are not the supreme beings of the universe; there are other more superior beings. They will become conscious of the reality that they are members of a large family having at the head, the First Son, the Christ, whom they will recognize on the ethereal plane. In their consciousness, a door will open and they will learn more about the elder brothers and sisters.

In the beginning, only a few people will perceive this reality, but eventually all of humanity will be touched by it. As Uranus is the master of Aquarius, it will bring great scientific discoveries, and people will become aware of the different types of energies animating their bodies. Uranus will help them understand that above all they are *energy*—and *light* is the fuel that nourishes their intelligence.

Moreover, in the fixed zodiac, there are three air signs: Aquarius, Gemini and Libra. We shall see three types of influence in the Aquarian epoch: we have already mentioned that Uranus is the master of Aquarius and its influence above; now Mercury is the master of Gemini and Venus, the master of Libra, these two will improve communication that will surpass anything known yet to date. It is said that, in this epoch, the human genius will reach its full potential. Venus in Libra will invite people to understand, to love each other, and to work for the well-being of all. One of the greatest

---

46 Omraam Mikhaël Aïvanhov, *A New Dawn: Society and Politics in the Light of Initiatic Science*, Part 1, Complete Works, Vol. 25, France, Prosveta S.A., ed. 1990, pages 36–37.

changes of this era will be at the level of the arts where music will show the best of human expression.

The manifestation of a cosmic plan can only happen through the process of time. The hierarchies of the higher regions in the invisible world cannot force human beings to infringe on the law of free will. Time will play its role, and everyone will come to learn at their own pace. Each human being will have to make his/her own decisions. It is only by recognizing the cosmic laws and through learning a new behavior that we can succeed. That is the basis of the teaching of Master Omraam Mikhaël Aïvanhov; he put behavior at the very foundation of his life.

Exercise: Take a moment of reflection to visualize this elder of Aquarius who pours the water of the new life over your entire being. This water brings you the inspiration, ability to adapt, and expansion that is harmonizing you with new currents descending from the Cosmos. Let yourself bathe and float in those energies.

The Water Bearer © Ivano Marchesani

CHAPTER 10
Melchizedek: Master of Masters

Christ and the Archangel Mikhaël are two different
ways of representing a unique Principle, the second
Principle of the Blessed Trinity. The solar entity that
we call Mikhaël is linked to the Christ, to the Word
of God, because the Spirit of Christ is the Spirit of
the Sun. And Melchizedek, he whom St. John saw
in the midst of seven golden lamps, holding seven
stars in his hand and with a sharp two-edged sword
from his mouth, is also an expression of the light, of
the Word. The names are different, but the principle
is the same.[47]

THE QUESTION HERE, IN the Apocalypse of St. John, is of a revelation
dictated by Melchizedek himself.

Speaking about the most mysterious being in this world is no
easy task because there is little said about this Being. He is like
the other spiritual face of the Christ principle: the one who never
incarnates and never dies—the one who has the power to manifest
Himself without incarnating.

---

47 Omraam Mikhaël Aïvanhov, *The fruits of the Tree of Life*, Complete
    Works, vol. 32, France, Prosveta S.A. ed. 1989, pp. 74–75.

The Bible, the Puranas, and the Vedas of ancient India are in agreement in stating that Melchizedek does not have a genealogy. He was not born from a mother or a father, and He was present even before man peopled the earth. He was named by the Eternal Priest of God Most High. This being will change His name throughout different epochs but His essence always remains the same. In the Hindu tradition, He is named Markandeya, Manu, and Son of the Sun, Brighu, Pramiti and Kalki, the tenth incarnation of Vishnu. He is also known as the Alpha and Omega, the beginning and the end.

There have been numerous misunderstandings regarding the Christ. The Christ is a cosmic, solar Spirit. The ability of fully manifesting within itself the science of the two principles—the eternal masculine and the eternal feminine—allows one to be adumbrated by the Spirit of Christ. The great Initiates are those Beings who have been able to do so. Jesus is such an example—as was Moses, Abraham, Krishna, Zoroaster, and many more. Therefore, Jesus is the historical person, but the Christ is a cosmic principle that manifested several times throughout the ages.

In the hierarchy order of the great Masters of humanity, the distinction, the highest, is that of the Priest of the Most High. This order to which all the Initiates belong has existed since the beginning of time. This order, the most sacred, is the order of Christ. Melchizedek himself, also known as the King of Justice and Peace, is the guardian of the tradition. The tradition speaks of the science of the two principles without which life could not exist or manifest itself.

In a lecture on December 28, 1958, Master Omraam Mikhaël Aïvanhov said:

> Consider how great is the One to whom the patriarch Abraham gave the tithing of everything. Have you ever thought of Melchizedek? Have you asked yourself the question who He was and what was the difference between Jesus and Himself? Melchizedek is a Priest without beginning or end. He therefore

existed before the creation of the world and human beings. He still exists. How did he then come to earth if he does not have a father or mother?

There you go my dear brothers and sisters, if you want to believe me, the information I am giving you comes from the Source. I have not been instructed by men. On earth, there is always a Being, created by God Himself, who is His representative throughout eternity. It is therefore Him who took the form of a body through his Spirit and who is the Spirit of God Himself, or if you prefer, of Christ. Since He is the Master of matter, He creates a form for Himself as the earth must not be deprived of a representative of God for ever. He is always present but throughout the centuries, His body changes, it renews itself and he gives it another name. He is present but does not bear the name of Melchizedek. He is precisely of the order of Christ. Christ and Melchizedek are the same in spirit. Christ existed before Jesus did.[48]
[our translation]

St. Paul, in the Epistle to the Hebrews in chapter 5, said that his Master, Jesus, was of the order of Melchizedek. And in chapter 7, it is said that Abraham was the first in the order and by being blessed by Him, he gave Him all his tithing. Melchizedek holds the power in the three worlds: physical, spiritual, and divine. Melchizedek, through the intermediary of Abraham, instituted the celebration of the wheat and the vine, symbols of the two principles. And during the Last Supper, Jesus transmitted it in his turn to his disciples through the bread and wine. The bread, or the body of Christ, can be understood as the symbol of wisdom, and the wine, the blood of Christ, as that of love. The two together produce Life or the Truth.

In *Man's Subtle Bodies and Centers*, Omraam Mikhaël Aïvanhov describes the following experience of Crookes:

---

48 This lecture was published by Prosveta in the French collection Vidélina, #19 under the title *"L'École de Melchisédek"*

When an electric current is applied between two electrodes in the tube, the cathode emits a flow of electrons in the direction of the anode. The cathode remains dark but the anode lights up. This experiment is an excellent illustration of the relationship between the masculine and the feminine principles. Everywhere, throughout the whole of nature, you can see these two principles at work. It is this *Initiatic Science* which Melchizedek revealed to Abraham: the existence of the two principles which manifest themselves in a multitude of different forms throughout the universe, and the manner in which they work together. [49]

Master Omraam Mikhaël Aïvanhov recommends associating this communion with the two principles while taking our daily meals. Supporting a vegetarian diet, he suggests eating in silence, with a heart filled with gratitude toward the Creator and the sun in order to make conscious exchanges with the food, which he called the "yoga of nutrition".

Knowing how to eat is learning how to love. In this way, by eating in a conscious manner, people have the possibility to transform the earth: all the elements going through their bodies are impregnated with love emanations, gratitude and sublime thoughts that shall remain in those particles. It is a basic and simple method repeated day after day and of communing with the two principles.

He also teaches us to go directly to the source of wisdom and love: the light and the warmth of the sun. Since the solar Entity is also the Spirit of Christ, each morning when the sun rises, it sends us his rays of infinite purity. Each day, at dawn, we can breathe the light of the sun—his wisdom, his warmth, and his love—thus perpetuating the teaching of Christ, that of the two principles.

---

49 Omraam Mikhaël Aïvanhov, *Man's Subtle Bodies and Centres*. Izvor Collection, #219, France, Prosveta S.A., ed. 1986, p. 89.

These are easy methods endowed with an incredible, immeasurable power.

Do you understand the importance of Melchizedek and what he has given to humanity?

In the sacred books of India, the Puranas and the Vedas, he is often associated with other Rishis. He always works in connection with a great Initiate. Brighu, the divine spark, creator of the races, is associated to Angiras, the flaming one. Later on, Markendeya, the immortal, will be associated to Vyasa, the clairvoyant, the erudite. It is said of Vyasa that he was the Light that guided the world. These two beings are like the two faces of the same coin. They come back in each epoch to help us in our evolution.

The coming of the Kalki Avatar is predicted for the end of the Kali Yuga and will bring on the sixth race—the race of the heart, that of love—which will create the next Golden Age. Some predictions have been described in the Vishnu Purana; in more ancient times, Markandeya Rishi explained how men during the four ages or yugas will fall away from the divine. Kali Yuga is the epoch in which we live presently. In this Age of Iron, men will only perceive through their physical senses and only think through their analytical minds. The coming of the Kalki Lord will help humanity to reintroduce the Golden Age it knew during the time of Ram, during the previous Satya Yuga.

Melchizedek will be Kalki, the Initiator of this Golden Age. He shall return with the seven Rishis. They will manifest in the world to eradicate evil. The Holy Grail will be found anew. He shall only come when the new man, instructed in the initiatic schools, will be ready to return to the heavenly home. When these times shall come, it will be the end of the illusion in which we live.

We must pass through purification before we can attain this Golden Age predicted at the dawn of time. We have profaned the sacred—and massacred millions of animals and people—for which there is a price to pay. The future is grandiose despite those tribulations, and a new earth and new heaven shall come. Symbolically speaking, this means that people will grow in love and wisdom because they shall understand the importance of the two principles. There will be only one worship, embracing all the great religious beliefs; it shall be the solar culture, that of Christ. He shall manifest again in a different manner—in our own consciousness.

It is said that, for one thousand years, evil will be banished to allow this evolution to take place. It will be time for humanity to live in justice and peace.

Men and women will be reconciled. They will have greater respect for each other as they will for Mother Nature. The science of the two principles on which the whole creation of the universe is based will be better understood, respected, and honored. The forces set in better balance will make the wheel of life turn harmoniously. Illnesses, famine, and wars will be banished. The good will prevail; joy, happiness, and true love will reign. The greed for money shall disappear and will be replaced by the desire to acquire the gold of the heart, the solar gold, inexhaustible and creator of life.

For this to happen, all men and women must unite and desire it profoundly in their hearts, in their thoughts and through their actions. Melchizedek must first come into the minds and the thoughts of all people.

Exercise: Let us imagine this extraordinary being that Melchizedek is, as described by St. John, who is the true King, Lord of Justice and Peace. He has the power to re-establish peace and harmony on earth. In looking at the sun, each day, let us pray with love that he comes to help humanity.

Melchizedek, Cathedral of Venice from sculptor Giovanni
Maria Morlaiter, photographed by Wolfgang Moroder

CHAPTER 11
Creating Unity among All Spiritualists

THE PURPOSE OF THIS chapter is to explore the idea of creating unity among all spiritualists. Materialists have often shown how powerful it is to unite forces and work together, hand in hand, in order to achieve their goals. Many have mastered, to a large degree, the art of putting aside differences, working together to find solutions to their problems to achieve success. If materialists generally succeed so well in whatever they choose to create, it is because they know where their interests lie. And many among them have understood that unity is the key to realizing their goals. Wonderful creations exist everywhere to remind us that materialists are indeed successful creators.

Why aren't most spiritualists taking this approach as an example? We often see spiritualists arguing about who is right or wrong and trying to prove that one philosophy or practice is better than another. One may wonder whether or not spiritualists know where their interests lie.

For centuries, religions have been critical of other religions and, in some cases, even fight violently against others with the conviction that anyone not sharing their belief system is unworthy or an enemy that must be eliminated. Anyone not practicing their rituals or speaking their "language" is seen as an outsider. In some cases, they even kill in the name of their religion; the Inquisition of the past and the extremists of today are only two examples.

Many spiritual leaders tell us that the time has come for people to realize that the apparent divisions between religions and various philosophies are actually a matter of perception; all religions, at their source, support the same principles and concepts. It is the human interpretation and the practices that bring division and separation.

Spiritualists should be working together for a better world—a world of unity and peace—by following the spirit of their teaching. Do we have to wait until everything crumbles around us—until we find ourselves completely powerless, unable to fix anything and utterly defenseless—before we instinctively ask for help from an invisible force or power? At that point, the invisible force that we may not comprehend—but desperately search for—becomes alive within us in the form of a feeling and an inner knowing. When this takes place, there can be no more ignorance that God is not within us all.

We do not sufficiently realize that truth exists in all religions—not only in the West, but also in the East—and in all spiritual movements. Jesus of Nazareth's mission in life was to teach the oneness of God, that life is eternal, and that there is no death in the realm of the soul and the spirit. These are the principles of spiritualism, and they should be a link in a spiritual chain to bind all people together in love.

It is time to move the energy from the intellect that divides and separates us to the energy of the heart, which is inclusive to all. Ammachi, a living Saint from Kerala, South India, teaches us by her own example to love and embrace everyone, regardless of religion or spiritual background. Ammachi travels tirelessly throughout the world, giving selfless and unconditional love by hugging countless people, radiating compassion, and demonstrating that only love can help solve problems.

Ammachi tells us that we all have that same potential. She wants to heal the heart of the world by simply giving and giving more love. She tells us that we can all connect to the same source of pure love that flows through her—like someone who is plugged into a high-voltage transformer that never shuts down.

If one person such as Ammachi is able to touch the hearts of millions of people from around the world by allowing divine love to flow through her and giving unconditional love to every single human being that comes to her, imagine what it would be like if all spiritualists decided to follow her example! If they would connect with divine love first—and then collectively unite by mentally focusing and connecting with one another to send out pure, impersonal thoughts and feelings of that divine love to all human beings on the planet—this would create a huge wave of divine power that could move mountains. People in darkness and spiritual ignorance would unknowingly feel this powerful outpouring of love. This would also create waves of spiritual awakening for those open to feeling it.

There is no doubt that there is a very strong spiritual current at the present time. Ernest Thompson, one of spiritualism's great pioneers, wrote that a spiritual revolution would sweep the earth and that man would enter a "spiritual age." Instead of material survival, spiritual survival would become the great incentive to progress.

Spiritualism has certainly led us to discover that what is believed to be the rare gift of Masters, Yogis, and Saints is actually a path open to those who are ready to make the pilgrimage to this inner sanctuary where spiritual illumination can be found. The surest path for spiritualists is to listen to their inner voices and to raise their vibrations to higher frequencies.

Spiritualists should emphasize to their fellow human beings the importance of finding the kingdom of heaven within. It should be their aim to clear away the misunderstandings and to present a new way of thinking and living that could bring the world a lasting peace and brotherhood: a Golden Age. This is certainly not an overnight undertaking, although, as we all know, no good end is achieved by imposing one's beliefs on others. This must be done by example, unity, truth, and love.

Omraam Mikhaël Aïvanhov says that present spiritual movements work for their own interests, thinking that they alone possess the truth, each one taking itself for the center of the universe, claiming to know more than the other movements, or to be more gifted, more powerful, or richer.[50] He continues saying that this mentality is no longer appropriate since we are entering the Age of Aquarius. If we want to move along with the changes that are occurring throughout nature and the Earth, we have to adopt a different attitude with the purpose of approaching unity through diversity.

Once there is an understanding among all spiritualists of the great benefit of uniting, working together, of having one goal in common—the realization of a Golden Age on Earth—then the dynamic is quite different. This Golden Age was once realized in the distant past; if all spiritualists know where those interests are, they can make it happen again. All Golden Ages shared a universal approach, a solar approach. We must move forward together toward a universal civilization as the sun shows us. The sun does not discriminate among different nationalities, races, or religions; it gives its light, warmth, and life to all people, regardless if one is Catholic, Protestant, Muslim, Hindu, or Buddhist. It is only to our benefit to become like the sun.

In the invisible realm, Sages, Initiates, and Masters are all members of the same family—the Universal Brotherhood—working together for the bettering of mankind. Edgar Cayce (1877–1945), the best-documented psychic healer of the twentieth century, also known as the Sleeping Prophet, spoke about this invisible organization as many others have.

It is now a great time for all spiritualists to unite and spread the message of love. We can maintain our identity, culture, and language, but—in the world of thoughts—we can unite and feel that we belong to the same family. We all share the same Father God and the same Mother Nature; we are all children of the same planet, of the universe. We must expand our consciousness by putting the small family into the big family.

Recent studies are adding to a growing body of evidence suggesting that focused prayers, especially those offered on a large scale, have a predictable and measurable effect on the quality of life during the time of the prayer. Scientists are now suspecting that the

---

50 Omraam Mikhaël Aïvanhov, *A philosophy of Universality*, Izvor Collection #206, France, Prosveta, ed. 1989, p. 132-133.

relationship between mass prayer and the activity of individuals in communities is, in fact, a phenomenon known as the "field effect" of consciousness.

Scientist Gregg Braden tells us that it has been proven, through experiments, that there is a field around us—a collective consciousness, in which we all participate and, therefore, have the power to change the world. This collective consciousness creates our reality and it can be influenced through our DNA by using the power of our thoughts and our hearts. He goes on to say that we can use this awareness on an individual basis to collectively change our world. Using principles recognized only recently in quantum physics, Braden demonstrates how Isaiah's nonreligious, nondenominational form of prayer transcends time and distance to bring healing to our bodies and peace to the nations of our modern world.[51]

Based on his theory of the Divine Matrix, he also discovered a formula—the square root of 1 percent—showing that the effect of thought influences the collective consciousness. He states that a determined number of participants would be needed to achieve a certain effect, like peace, for instance. His experiments have proven the validity of his formula.[52] For example, to lift the consciousness of the world's population, it would only require some 8,000 participants concentrating on the same idea of peace. The power of visualization is a gift from God for mankind to take our fate into our own hands instead of standing by and watching powerlessly. So, let's accept this gift gratefully and use it constructively.

The threads that weave all spiritualists together, regardless of particulars and principles, bind us together. At the dawning of a new day, may we find a common ground among ourselves and work together for the greater good of mankind. May we stand together in strength and conviction. May peace and harmony reign in our hearts. And may we have the wisdom to put aside our differences and quicken our collective awakening in order for us all to become benefactors of humanity.

---

51 Gregg Braden *"The Isaiah Effect: Decoding the Lost Science of Prayer and Prophecy"* USA, Three Rivers Press, 2000.

52 http://spiritlibrary.com/gregg-braden/the-lost-mode-of-prayer

In *Light is a Living Spirit,* Master Omraam Mikhaël Aïvanhov gives a powerful collective exercise called the spiritual laser. Based on the definition of the word laser (Light Amplification by Stimulated Emission of Radiations), he describes that the power of the laser resides in the fact that the particles (photons) are all vibrating at the same frequency, producing a monochromatic light in the same direction in specific phases. These produce a coherent light of extraordinary power. From this reality, he goes to say that Sages of the past knew about the laser well before science discovered it and that if human beings decided to all vibrate together on the same wavelength or subject— Light, they could form a powerful laser that could be used to uplift humanity. However, before participating in this collective endeavor, he recommends that preliminary inner preparation for everyone is the key:

> Every human being possesses a spirit, a soul, an intellect, a heart, a will and a physical body, and the great difficulty lies in getting them all to work in unison with each other. No one can be strong or powerful until he achieves inner unity, and one of the goals of initiation is to create this harmony in man.[53]

Paramahansa Yogananda, another spiritual Master, tells us the following: "Focus your attention within. You will feel a new power, a new strength, a new peace—in body, mind and spirit."[54]

John J. Delaney wrote the following:

> When we look at the world as a great wagon wheel of which we are the spokes and God is the hub, it becomes clear that our first task is to remain

---

53 Omraam Mikhaël Aïvanhov, *Light is a Living Spirit*, Izvor collection #212, France Prosveta, ed. 1987, p. 131.

54 Paramahansa Yogananda, *"Where there is Light"*, USA, Self Realization Fellowship, 1998, p. 6.

anchored to the hub. There, in the center, we find
ourselves most closely connected with each other.
From that center in which we are all rooted the force
comes forth to make that wheel turn.[55]

Moreover, other spiritual teachers emphasize the necessity
of connecting with the Divine within before acting on anything
external.

The great mystic saint of North India, Neem Karoli Babaji, said
that we can't realize God if we are aware of differences and that we
must learn to find the love within, to see the Lord in everyone. He
said that all religions are the same and that they all lead to God,
that God is everybody.[56]

If all spiritualists understood where their interests lie, and if they
decided to work together to form a large, universal family sending
out powerful waves of love and light, they would inspire and uplift
the general consciousness, and world peace could be achieved. Is this
feasible? Yes, absolutely.

The power of the laser resides in all the particles vibrating together
on the same wavelength at the same time. So, if all spiritualists
decided to unite at a particular moment, holding the same idea of the
light, the effect thus amplified could reach the whole world and help
every human being. It is a simple, powerful, and effective method.
Everyone would feel the support of the others vibrating on the same
wavelength or frequency. This would produce a beam of light of an
indescribable potency for the benefit of all—thanks to the effort of
uniting and working together.

When spiritualists realize that it is more beneficial to put aside
differences, to symbolically hold hands, and work together on the
same wavelength toward the same ideal of love and light, they will
be able to manifest harmony, love, and joy in the world in a very
powerful way.

In the same way as scientists unite to be heard by the masses,
spiritualists can have a wider impact on people once they show that

---

55   http://www.medium2000.org/The%20Higginson_files.htm
56   Ram Dass, *Miracle of Love*, E.P. Dutton, New York, 1979, p. 346

they are capable of achieving results in the physical world by uniting together on a single idea.

Exercise: If you have the blessing of belonging to a meditation or prayer group, or even if you are by yourself, we suggest the Spiritual Laser exercise:

At a chosen time, prepare yourself by being comfortable and relaxed. Mentally, create a link with the Elders on High and all the other people on earth who share your aspiration of unity. Then, inwardly harmonize your thinking and feeling by lighting up your inner lamp, expanding in that light. Mentally unite with one another and, in your mind's eye, concentrate on the white light (or the light of the sun). Envelop one another in that light. Bathe in that light. Vibrate in that light. Envelop the whole world in the light. Everyone is emitting the light and vibrating in the light. Together, you will form a ray of light as powerful as a laser and be capable of transforming and uplifting humanity.

Rays of Light © Claude Brun

CHAPTER 12

A Golden Age

WE HAVE ALREADY SPOKEN about a new Earth. This Earth cannot foresee a day without a new consciousness, which means a collection of beings awakened to their spirituality, conscious of their subtle bodies, their soul, and their spirit. The knowledge, acquisition, and use of psychic abilities will reveal the true reality. This change must first take place within a person—and then be transposed into their behavior.

This awakening of consciousness leads us to follow through with our development on all levels so that we can become the New Jerusalem: an awakened being, with its twelve doors open to connect with Heaven. The pearls and precious stones that St. John speaks of in the Apocalypse are the symbol of the purity and virtues of this New Jerusalem, the new awakened being in full expression.

In the past, we thought we were as dust and meant to return to dust—to remain humble and small. There was such a gap between us, God and the Christ, but the church said we could actually know both only through her. That was the church of St. Peter. However, there were many Saints, Prophets, Initiates and Sages who understood differently and have actually become Sons and Daughters of God. They have followed the precepts of Jesus: "Be you perfect as the Celestial Father is perfect!" and "Thy will be done on Earth as it is in Heaven!"

As prescribed by St. John in his reference to the New Jerusalem and by Hermes Trismegistus in his formula: "What is below must be like what is above", we are invited to improve, evolve, and reach perfection. We must not be separated from below (matter) or on high (spirit) but take care of both to make the miracle of our true nature happen.

When consciousness is awakened in someone, he/she realizes that the body is a living temple as well as all of nature. It is every day, not only the *seventh day*, that the awakened person works for the coming of the Kingdom of God and His righteousness. It is no longer a matter between external temples or churches but of everyone honoring their Higher Self within.

> "My Father is still working, and I also am working," said Jesus. Initiates, whose conscience is awakened, take part each day in God's work, as did Jesus and you too can take part in it. You will say, "But how can we, who are so ignorant and weak, participate in the work of God?"
>
> I shall give you a method. First of all, remain a long while in silence and in stillness, and then begin to elevate yourself through your thoughts. Imagine you are gradually leaving your body through the opening at the top of your skull. Keep imagining yourself rising through your causal, buddhic and atmic bodies, linking to the universal Soul, the cosmic principle that fills all of space and, there, participating in its work at all points of the universe simultaneously. Although you may not know clearly what you are doing, your spirit will know.[57]

We are all brothers and sisters on the planet. And nature, that we honor and respect because she is our living, nurturing Mother, becomes as sacrosanct as our body.

---

57 Omraam Mikhaël Aïvanhov, *Daily Meditations*, France, Prosveta S.A., 2011, p. 95, March 29, 2012.

As with the example of Jesus answering the Samaritan:

> Woman, believe me, the hour cometh, when you
> shall neither on this mountain, nor yet at Jerusalem,
> worship the Father. But the hour cometh, and now,
> is when the true worshippers shall worship the
> Father in spirit and in truth.[58]

Humanity is at a turning point in its development. Some beings are preparing themselves to become the bearers of peace and light. The suffering of people purifies and renews them so they welcome within themselves divine love. Each of us must become like the luminous rays of a new dawn.

When the collectivity of awakened beings becomes a fraternity, peace can prevail between the different religions and nations. Truth will be revealed from the depth of their being.

When man listens, God speaks,
When man obeys, God acts,
When men change, nations change. [59]

In the future, the aspect of work and time-management will be dealt with differently—it won't be as strenuous—and priorities will be reoriented toward self-development, inner work, and inspiration for art. It will no longer be a question of money and productivity but of developing a state of consciousness.

As mentioned previously, Ram established a Golden Age that lasted for several centuries. If civilizations in the past have known this Golden Age, why can't it happen again in the future? One thing these civilizations often had in common was a solar culture. This consideration for the sun is quite inspiring as the sun is the best example and model of our inner structure, of disinterestedness, of unconditional love: it gives its light and warmth to all beings,

---

58 Bible: Gospel of St. John, 4:21–23.
59 Peter Deunov, excerpt from a prayer entitled "The disciple morning prayer"

regardless of their race, color, or culture. It is the symbol of our own spirit: luminous, radiant, and vibrant. The sun is the initiator of our Higher Self. It is the best Master, impersonal and perfect, inviting us to imitate it.

> If you want to know what true morality is, you must learn from the sun; no one else can teach it. Human beings are always eager to tell you what you should do, but they are incapable of putting their own advice into practice; whereas the sun says nothing, his deeds speaks for him. He never says, "You must love your enemies." He never says, "I love you." No, but he goes on loving everyone all the time. Only the sun can teach us how to discover and respect the moral laws of the cosmos.[60]

If all aspects of human organization—politics, economy, education, or art—adopted the solar model, all frontiers, misery, and wars would disappear.

A new solar philosophy would bring new forms for sure, as Spirit is always seeking new forms to manifest itself, but the eternal and unchangeable principles of Christ—light, love, and goodness—will remain the same. This new solar approach will have a universal and perfect form so that the Spirit will come dwell in it and vivify it. That is why all the efforts we make to support the spirit rather than the letter, which means developing the qualities and virtues instead of the old forms, will bring us closer to this great brotherhood of the invisible world helping humanity in its evolution.

> The new step for the human culture and consciousness is now the fraternity between nations. All the people on earth will unite in such a way that the great will protect the weak and thus the fighting between nations will stop. The people of each country must

---

60 Omraam Mikhaël Aïvanhov, *A New Dawn: Society and Politics in the Light of Initiatic Science*, Vol. 26, France, Prosveta S.A., ed. 1999, p. 51.

make the effort to be great in Spirit through wisdom and love, and not through conquest and domination over the weakest. This means that the new world organization must support the great natural law: Life for all.[61]

In the human body, each organ works unselfishly for the well-being of the whole body. In the same way, each person and each nation should learn to work for the well-being of everyone.

The way in which the intelligence of nature has designed and constructed human beings teaches us an important lesson. If a person is fit and healthy, it is because all his organs are willing to live and work together in an unselfish spirit of brotherhood and generosity. If all the countries in the world did the same, the Kingdom of God would be possible.[62]

This chapter is an intense calling to consider our future with a new hope. With the knowledge and discovery of our inner true nature and all its possibilities, it proposes a great future. It invites us to rediscover the image of ourselves that has always existed in the depth of our souls.

Exercise: Create an image of yourself where the light and the splendor emanate from your cells. Feel your divine spark penetrate your consciousness and become one with it. You are guided, supported, enlightened, and vivified by the presence of your Higher Self. Your aura grows in strength and luminous colors as you practice this exercise every day. Observe the marvelous changes that will take place within.

---

61 Peter Deunov, *Wisdom: The Sixth Race, the Foundation of Universal Brotherhood*, France, Grain de Blé, 1968, p. 247 (translated from the French edition).

62 Omraam Mikhaël Aïvanhov, *A New Dawn: Society and Politics in the Light of Initiatic Science*, Complete Works, Vol. 26, France, Prosveta S.A., ed. 1999, p. 207.

Aura

Epilogue

In this book, dear reader, we spoke about the actual conditions on the planet that affect our daily life—in the political arena, the economy, nature, art, and evolution. Our goal was to look at the future in a broader sense, a possibility for a new life. For some, this represents a quantum leap; for others, it is an opening of hope or a life they have already been putting into practice.

Humanity has accomplished giant steps in the realms of science and communication thanks to the development of our intellectual faculties. Imagine what the future would be if we developed the qualities of the soul and the spirit! The marvels that await us are incredible.

It was said that Einstein's mental capacity was developed to just 10 percent of its human potential. Most of us achieve well below that percentage. Imagine if we fully developed our potential, to 100 percent: we could surely accomplish miracles! To achieve this, it is necessary that we learn about our complete structure including our subtle bodies. This is what meant the old adage: *Know Thyself,* i.e. know your Higher Self. For this to take place, we must adapt and be willing to learn the wisdom of *initiatic science.*

We can become living Emerald Tablets. Hermes Trismegistus said, "That which is below is as that which is above, and that which is above is as that which is below, to perform the miracles of the one thing."

Let us wish with all our hearts to create a new life—a Golden Age realized in the past that could become our future. It is no longer the quality of beings that is needed but the quantity that must decide and wish for it. Dedicate a couple of minutes each day to think about this noble ideal by linking with all those on the planet who vibrate on the same wavelength and want to spread Light on earth. This exercise contributes to create a New Heaven! And finally, adopt new behaviors in harmony with this desire to live a new life thus contributing to create a New Earth!

We are at the dawn of a new life that comes down from Heaven where the cosmic light will shine through our intelligence and universal love will emanate from our hearts. We can all become builders of the New Life.*

> *A human being cannot erase the past or change the present, but he has the power to create the future: it is God that gave him this power. His first vocation is to become a creator. In working with his thoughts, his feelings, and his actions according to the rules of initiatic science, he is capable of creating for himself, his children, and all of humanity a future of peace, light, and joy.*[63]

—The Aquarian Team

*By the New Life, we mean a life more conscious, where everyone pays more attention to their thinking, feelings, and actions, so harmony dwells within and reaches out to all humanity. The members of the Aquarian team are disciples of the teaching[64] of Omraam Mikhaël Aïvanhov, a spiritual Master born at the beginning of the twentieth century in Bulgaria, who spread his teaching orally mainly in France for more than half a century. Many references exist on the website of Prosveta or short clips on YouTube. We also invite you to obtain a copy of a new film entitled "In a Master's presence" through Amazon.ca.

---

63 According to the teaching of Omraam Mikhaël Aïvanhov and published on a bookmark by Prosveta S.A.

64 The conferences given by Master Aïvanhov for nearly half a century are being published by Prosveta S.A. in several languages. Visit their website: www.prosveta.com.

Acknowledgments

We, the Aquarian Team, are filled with gratitude for the learning we have received through the years by the teaching of Omraam Mikhaël Aïvanhov.

Prosveta S.A. for allowing us to use numerous quotes taken from their publications.

A great thank you to the editing team: Anne, David, Shannon, Pierre, and all those who have given us time and support for the great experience of writing this book.

Thank you to Balboa Press, our families, and our friends, all of whom accepted this project with open hearts and minds.

After receiving an inspired meditation at sunrise one day in 2011, Carmen Froment, asked a few of her close friends if they would like to assist her with writing this book, in a 'collective' way. We sincerely thank her for the trust she embodied form the beginning of this journey. Without her determination, endless support, and hard work, this book would not have seen the light of day! A profound thank you from the entire team.

About the Authors

The collection of ideas, subjects, and research for this book is the fruit of a team effort: nine authors and four proofreaders/editors worked together to make it ripe. The authors have studied the initiatic teachings of Omraam Mikhaël Aïvanhov for a combined number of approximately 279 years. They live on several continents.

Thank you to all the authors who accepted and gracefully participated in this project. They are listed here in alphabetical order:

Denise Bertrand: Canadian. International director, writer, and producer of drama programs and shows for youth.

Claude Brun: Okanagan Valley, British Columbia, Canada. Artist, photographer, researcher.

Rolff Désiré : Ottawa, Canada. Sales representative.

Carmen Froment : Kelowna, British Columbia, Canada. Flight attendant.

France Gilbert : Victoria, British Columbia, Canada. Accountant.

Richard Kamendje : Austria. UN, physicist.

Mark Walker: Kelowna, British Columbia, Canada. Entrepreneur-corporate owner.

Christiane van Aken: Sydney, Australia. Accountant.

Mikhaël van Aken: Sydney, Australia. Entrepreneur.